GREAT IMAGES
OF THE 20th CENTURY

TIME GREAT IMAGES

Editor	Kelly Knauer
Art Director	Anthony Wing Kosner
Picture Editors	Patricia Cadley, Dot McMahon
Associate Picture Editor	Robert Stephens
Associate Art Director	Scott G. Weiss
Research Director	Denise Lynch
Copy Editor	Bruce Christopher Carr
Production Director	John Calvano
Photo Technology	Urbano Delvalle
TIME Special Projects Editor	Barrett Seaman

Thanks to: Ames Adamson, Andy Blau, Anne Considine, Elena Falaro, Brian Fellows, Christina Scalet, Michael Skinner, Michele Stephenson, Cornelis Verwaal, Miriam Winocur

TIME INC. HOME ENTERTAINMENT

President	David Gitow
Director, Continuities and Single Sales	David Arfine
Director, Continuities and Retention	Michael Barrett
Director, New Products	Alicia Longobardo
Director, Licensing	Risa Turken
Group Product Manager	Jennifer McLyman
Product Managers	Roberta Harris, Carlos Jiminez, Kenneth Maehlum, Daniel Melore
Manager, Retail and New Markets	Thomas Mifsud
Associate Product Managers	Daria Raehse, Dennis Sheehan, Meredith Shelley, Betty Su, Niki Viswanathan, Lauren Zaslansky, Cheryl Zukowski
Assistant Product Managers	Victoria Alfonso, Jennifer Dowell
Editorial Operations Director	John Calvano
Book Production Manager	Jessica McGrath
Assistant Book Production Manager	Jonathan Polsky
Book Production Coordinator	Kristen Travers
Fulfillment Director	Michelle Gudema
Associate Fulfillment Manager	Richard Perez
Financial Director	Tricia Griffin
Financial Manager	Amy Maselli
Assistant Financial Manager	Steven Sandonato
Marketing Assistant	Ann Gillespie

Copyright 1999 by Time Inc. Home Entertainment
Published by TIME Books
Time Inc., 1271 Ave. of the Americas, New York, NY 10020

We welcome your comments and suggestions about TIME Books. Please write to us at:

TIME Books
Attention: Book Editors
P.O. Box 11016
Des Moines, IA 50336-1016

To order additional copies, please call 1-800-327-6388
(Monday through Friday 7:00 a.m.–8:00 p.m. or Saturday 7:00 a.m.–6:00 p.m. Central Time)

Printed in the United States of America

TIME
GREAT IMAGES
OF THE 20th CENTURY

THE PHOTOGRAPHS THAT DEFINE OUR TIMES

CONTENTS

TO ADVOCATE

80 The image loves to argue. In offering their differing accounts of the news, words reason, while images plead. Committed photographers have made their silent medium speak for the voiceless, from child workers to Dust Bowl Okies to AIDS patients.

TO RISK

98 Combat photography earned its stripes in the tumultuous 1930s and flourished in the epic battles of World War II. Later the cold war, Vietnam and a host of brush fires offered historic stages for these reporters-with-cameras— even as a new breed, the storm chasers, dared to record nature's fury.

TO EXPLORE

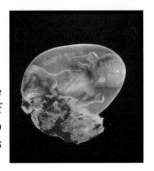

116 To scientists, cameras are machines for learning, and the range of visible light is only one of many ways to experience nature. Here are pictures that opened doors, eyes and minds.

TO REVEAL

134 TIME's two founders believed that history is driven by individuals. And we believe that, even in a world that has become ever more visually managed, gifted photographers can still uncover character traits that elude the eye.

TO CHEER

152 Here's a puzzle: Why do so few lasting sports photographs show Great Moments in Sports? Passing by the record breakers, the buzzer beaters and the sudden-death overtimes, the photo shopper in search of enduring athletic images may end up browsing in the adjacent aisles of politics, propaganda and the cold war.

THE INFORMING

ROY STRYKER IS ONE OF THE GREAT figures of American photography, even though he was an economist, not a cameraman. In 1935 President Franklin Roosevelt plucked him from teaching at Columbia University to run a New Deal program that is known to history as the Farm Security Administration. In this post, Stryker hired a legion of dedicated photojournalists—including Dorothea Lange, Ben Shahn, Arthur Rothstein and others—who compiled a magnificent visual chronicle of American farm life during the Depression. Later, in reviewing the more than 270,000 pictures produced by his team, Stryker wrote, "It is called a great collection now, perhaps the greatest ever assembled in the history of America. But I am not interested in adjectives. I am only interested in pictures."

It's a fine observation, Stryker's way of saying that trying to comprehend pictures through words is a bad idea, as futile as explaining mathematics by singing. Since the editors of this book agree with Stryker, readers will find that the text accompanying the pictures in these pages is intended primarily to provide information about the photographs and the events they record rather than to analyze and interpret the images themselves.

In exploring the many ways in which the photograph acts as an information device, the book follows the definition of news used by TIME editors since 1923: news is more than the affairs of national politics and world events, important as they are. News also arrives in the revelations of science and in the evolutions of society, from cloning to moon rocks to rock fests. And since TIME has long believed that history is shaped not by faceless forces of politics and economics but rather by the acts of powerful men and women, the book also includes revealing pictures of the century's significant newsmakers.

Because the volume focuses on the picture in its role as town crier, many schools of photography are not featured here. There are no fashion photographs, no art photographs and no formal portraits. There are no funny animal pictures and no human-interest pictures. Instead, the emphasis is on the historic pictures that constitute a visual map of our times—and on a

EYE

Technology turned cameras into town criers, and—in a flash—a medium that defined our century was born

few lesser-known pictures that shed a revealing light on the ways and days of life in the 20th century. Rather than trying to find a picture to illustrate every significant moment of the century, we have concentrated on pictures that are great on their own terms, those that endure in our minds as icons of the times.

The volume's chapters reflect the many ways photographers use cameras to bring us the news, beginning with the most basic function of the news picture: to witness and record historic events. Subsequent chapters explore more specific aspects of this task. One features photos that captured events at the exact instant they occurred, such as Eddie Adams' photo (opposite page) of the summary execution of a suspected Vietcong officer. Another collects a gallery of pictures produced under extreme risk, like storm-chaser J. Pat Carter's shot of an advancing tornado threatening a mother and two young children (above). Major sections are also devoted to photographers who use the camera to advocate social change, and to photographers who use the camera with a historian's eye, to document our social life.

Since TIME considers science to be one of history's driving forces, the book also explores the many ways that scientists have used the photograph as a tool of discovery. Here we find pictures that offer new ways of experiencing reality, from infrared and ultraviolet wavelengths to satellite photographs. In some cases, these new ways of seeing have given us new ways of being: it is no accident that Earth Day was inaugurated only a few years after mankind first saw a picture of the whole earth suspended in space. As Apollo 8 astronaut Jim Lovell remarked, "the vast loneliness up here ... makes you realize just what you have back there on earth."

But technology is not simply one aspect of photojournalism; in many ways it is its parent. At the turn of the century, photographs played an important role as a documentary medium: they took America's portrait and revealed its vast landscapes. They were becoming political tools, as well: at the end of the 19th century, Jacob Riis had shown that photographs could document horrifying social conditions and argue for their reform. But camera shutters were still not fast enough to capture action, only its effects.

&&The 270,000 pictures [of the Farm Security Administration
in the history of America. But I am not interested in adjective

The early decades of the new century saw such historic upheavals as World War I and the Russian Revolution—only readers *didn't* see them. In the Great War, censors prevented cameramen, on pain of death, from recording the slaughter at the front lines, showing that politicians recognized the power of the picture long before Lyndon Johnson blamed combat photographers for Americans' dwindling support for the conflict in Vietnam.

But there was a more compelling reason for the paucity of action photographs early in the century: good cameras were still bulky and hard to handle. The revolution that made photojournalism a reality came when lighter, faster cameras and portable flash systems were developed. Now cameras were mobile, footloose. And the pictures they took were candid and spontaneous. Alfred Eisenstaedt's first photographs, which seemed to capture real life on film, startled readers accustomed to stagey, stuffy poses. And even as these breakthrough images began to appear, advances in printing allowed the photos to reach a mass audience more quickly, and with better reproduction quality.

Suddenly, pictures were news, and soon new publications were developed to feature this powerful new form of journalism. First introduced in Europe, the picture-driven magazine took America by storm when TIME co-founder Henry Luce introduced LIFE in 1936. Though Roy Stryker had his quarrels with the new magazines, he recalled the heady feeling of the period: "In 1936 photography, which theretofore had been mostly a matter of landscapes and snapshots and family portraits, was fast being discovered as a serious tool of communications."

THE TIME WAS RIGHT FOR THIS NEW information medium. For just as great poetry demands great audiences, memorable photographs demand historic events to record. Photojournalism thrived in the tempestuous '30s and through the epic battles of World War II. Combat photographers like Robert Capa threw themselves into the front lines to capture war in close-up, becoming heroes to readers. TIME covered the war in a symbiotic relationship with its sister publication

LIFE, with TIME handling the words and LIFE the pictures. When read together, as Henry Luce intended, the two publications offered a rich account of the week's news, uniting the sheer impact of the picture with the precision and depth of the word.

When Paris was liberated in 1944, the jeep that followed General Jacques Leclerc into the city carried a typical TIME-LIFE team: TIME writer Charles Christian Wertenbaker and LIFE photographer Robert Capa. Months later, when Capa parachuted into hostile territory with U.S. paratroopers, his account of his exploits ran as a feature article in TIME—sans pictures.

In its role as a digest of the week's news, TIME has always run historic pictures, including many Pulitzer-prizewinning newspaper photos. But it was only after the demise of LIFE as a weekly publication in 1972 that TIME began to feature more color in its pages and to put first-rate photographers on its staff. Under picture editor Arnold Drapkin in the 1970s and '80s and current picture chief Michele Stephenson, TIME has become a leading forum for news photography. Veteran photojournalists like Dirck Hal-

stead, Diana Walker and P.F. Bentley are among the finest chroniclers of national politics, while James Nachtwey, Christopher Morris and Anthony Suau have braved fire in hot spots around the world to take award-winning pictures of war and rebellion. They are worthy successors to the great photojournalists of the mid-century.

Yet photojournalism, which has richly documented the historic events of the 20th century, finds itself in some danger as the century ends, a victim of the same force—technology—that gave it life. Once the picture was an undisputable source of truth; now any photograph can be scanned into a computer and altered to provide a convincing image of a reality that never existed. Just as photographs have defined our century, the century itself may end up being defined as the last era when the truth of a photograph was accepted unequivocally.

Even so, we suspect that readers a century from now will still enjoy the pictures of great photojournalists, as we hope today's readers will enjoy this gallery of our time's most compelling photos. But that's enough adjectives. Turn the page, and look at the pictures. ▪

WITNESS

A YOUNG Vietnamese girl, Phan Thi Kim Phuc, runs down a road in agony, her skin aflame with the jellied gasoline called napalm. She has torn off her burning clothing. Most people who look at this picture have seen it before; have seen it so frequently that it has become an icon, a sort of visual mental shorthand, an image that perfectly encapsulates an idea—in this case, the cruelty of war and the futility of America's involvement in Vietnam.

How many people saw this event? Ten? Twenty? Yet because photographer Nick Ut was there to record the scene, the nine-year-old's plight haunts the memories of millions who never saw her burn. In that magnification of impact lies the magic of photography and the mission of photojournalism. In our time the camera has become a lever long enough to move the world.

Pictures bear witness. Pictures testify. Pictures say, This happened, in just this way, at just this time. But a picture is also mute: it can't account for what it shows us. So pictures demand explaining. The commander of U.S. forces in Vietnam couldn't deny this image, so he tried to pass it off as "a hibachi accident." In fact, the napalm that scorched Kim Phuc was "friendly fire," dropped from South Vietnamese planes that were trying to stop North Vietnamese troops from attacking her village.

Pictures have another limitation: as cross-sections of time, they can't tell us what happened next. In our minds, Kim Phuc will run forever down that road. But her life went on: she healed, married and finally defected to Canada. "I have to show [my son] what happened to his mom, to her country, and that there should never be war again," she told LIFE photographer Joe McNally in 1995. It might be the credo of the photojournalist: I will bear witness, even to things you may not wish to see. "I have to show." ∎

"With all the arguments and discussions about the Vietnam War, what did the visual image do? It ended the war.**"** – CORNELL CAPA

CHILDREN FLEEING A NAPALM ATTACK IN VIETNAM, 6/8/72
Huynh Cong ("Nick") Ut

ON STRIKE!

In 1999 labor leader Walter P. Reuther was named one of the TIME 100, the magazine's list of the most influential people of the 20th century. In his profile of Reuther, longtime labor leader Irving Bluestone notes that photographs of the beating of Reuther and his associates by Ford Motor Co. goons in 1937 were a major factor in winning public sympathy for the union agenda.

Four years later, the tables were turned: in this picture, members of the the automobile workers' union, on strike at the giant Ford plant in River Rouge, Mich., are attacking a man who refused to stop working and join their picket line. The victim covers his head with his coat to soften their blows.

This picture earned Milton Brooks of the Detroit *News* the first Pulitzer Prize ever given for news photography. These awards, the brainchild of newspaper mogul Joseph Pulitzer, were founded in 1918. In establishing an award for photography, the Pulitzer committee recognized the growing role of the picture as a source of news. The Pulitzers are restricted to newspaper journalism; many of the pictures in this book are Pulitzer winners, but many others were never eligible, having first appeared in TIME, LIFE and other magazines.

**VIOLENCE ON THE
PICKET LINE, 4/3/41**
Milton Brooks

THE HORROR

The century's most profound crimes were revealed in the spring of 1945, as Allied troops liberated the dread death camps of Adolf Hitler's Reich. LIFE photographer George Rodger, a Briton, took this picture at the Bergen-Belsen camp. It is brutal in its incongruity: the boy seems matter-of-fact as he strolls past the bodies of the victims—yet we note his gaze is firmly turned away from the grisly scene. Rodger's own notes from that day: "Dead lying by the side of one of the roads in the camp. They die like this in the thousands. When they became so weak they could no longer walk they just lay down & died ..." Those who survived the Holocaust often had no homes to return to, like the pair of orphaned Polish Jews at right, who had just been denied permission to enter Palestine.

**LIBERATION OF
BERGEN-BELSEN, 4/45**
George Rodger

TO WITNESS

Left:

**KOREANS FLEE
PYONGYANG BY
BRIDGE, 12/50**
Max Desfor

**DEATH AT THE
BERLIN WALL, 8/62**
Photographer Unknown

NO EXIT

The long struggle known as the cold war was a new sort of conflict: it erupted into real warfare—often fought by proxy armies—at a host of pressure points around the perimeter of Winston Churchill's "Iron Curtain."

In June 1950 North Korean troops crossed the 38th parallel and invaded South Korea. United Nations troops, largely made up of U.S. forces, joined the conflict, rolling the North Koreans back and capturing their capital, Pyongyang. But then the Chinese army entered the fray, driving the U.N. troops into retreat.

In December, AP photographer Max Desfor found hundreds of Koreans outside Pyongyang fleeing the communist forces by crossing a bombed-out bridge that had collapsed into the Taedong River. "The people were half frozen," said Desfor. The picture was awarded the Pulitzer Prize.

Twelve years later, the flight from communism was echoed in miniature at a new fault line of the cold war: the Berlin Wall. When East German youth Peter Fechter, 18, was killed during an attempt to escape through the wall, a soldier carried his body back in a grim pietà.

TO WITNESS

Right:
**GRIEVING STUDENT AT KENT
STATE UNIVERSITY, 5/4/70**
John Paul Filo

**THE ASSASSINATION OF
ROBERT F. KENNEDY, 6/5/68**
Bill Eppridge

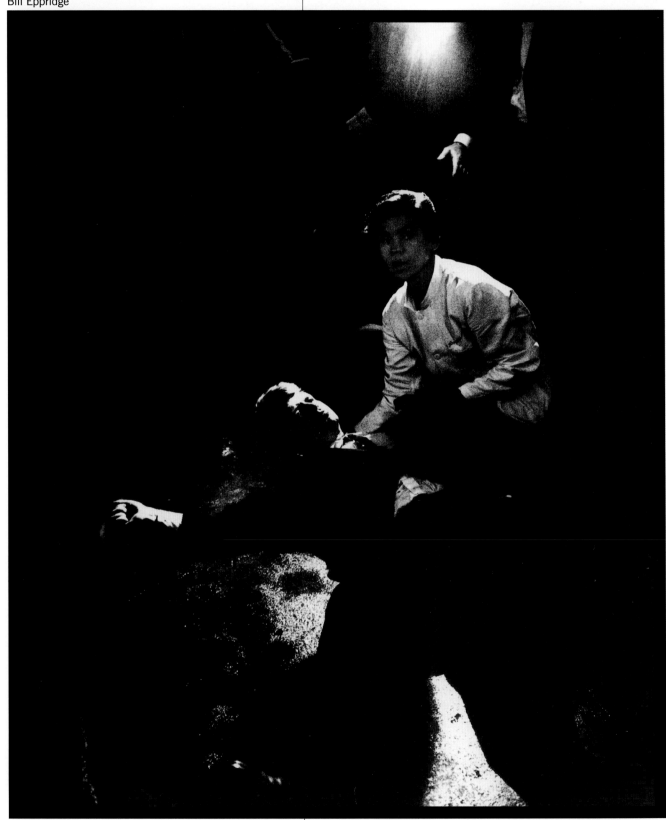

A TIME FOR ELEGIES

America's turbulent 1960s and early '70s survive in a series of still images that have become icons of the age. Here are two of them:

In June 1968 LIFE photographer Bill Eppridge was on hand when Senator Robert F. Kennedy, vying for the Democratic presidential nomination, was shot by Sirhan Sirhan in the kitchen of Los Angeles' Ambassador hotel. The busboy in the picture is Juan Romero, then 17, who recalled the event 30 years later for TIME. Romero had met Kennedy the night before, after angling to take a room-service call to the senator; the Kennedys were heroes of Romero's family in Mexico. Romero recalls cradling the dying man: "I swear Mr. Kennedy said either, 'Is everybody O.K.?' or 'Everything's going to be O.K.'"

In May 1970 John Paul Filo was a photography student taking pictures for the school yearbook at Ohio's Kent State University when members of the Ohio National Guard shot and killed four students protesting the Vietnam War. "I didn't react visually," Filo recalled of taking this Pulitzer prizewinning image. "This girl came up and knelt over the body and let out a God-awful scream that made me click the camera." That scream—silent in the photograph—still reverberates.

This century, said TIME co-founder Henry Luce, is "the American Century." The nation's balance-tipping entry into World War I, its leadership of the Allied cause in World War II and its successful struggle against the Soviet Union in the cold war were high points of its journey from isolationism to a commanding role as the world's undisputed superpower.

But there were low points as well— and this image is perhaps the most ignominious of them, a haunting presence in the American mind. The year is 1975; the month is April; the scene is the roof of a building near the U.S. embassy in Saigon. U.S. helicopters are airlifting American citizens and pro-U.S. South Vietnamese out of the besieged city, even as victorious troops of the North Viet-namese army are entering its outskirts. An undeclared war that had claimed more than 58,000 American lives—and turned the nation into a bitter, divided land— is ending with a whimper.

The airlift operation lasted about 21 hours, with helicopters landing on the roofs of several Saigon buildings; the final flights were from the top of the American embassy. In 1995, on the 20th anniversary of the airlift, TIME interviewed some of those who had participated in it. Kenneth Moorefield, a Foreign Service officer and former infantry captain, recalled his last look around the embassy: "Hundreds of Vietnamese had swarmed over the walls and were looting … Some were driving embassy cars around and around in almost a maniacal frenzy. On the other side of the walls, crowds were shouting chants against the U.S., celebrating the imminent victory of the communists."

EVACUATING SAIGON, 4/29/75
Hubert Van Es

ARMS AND THE MAN

In the spring of 1989, Chinese students gathered in Beijing's Tiananmen Square to mourn the death of political reformer Hu Yaobang. For seven weeks they occupied the square, demanding freedom and democracy for all Chinese.

On June 4, the government sent tanks against the protesters. As the world watched on television, a lone figure stopped one column of tanks for six minutes—and left behind a visual image that has come to embody the struggle of one man against the massive, faceless power of state machinery.

The man was never identified; some say he was 19-year-old student Wang Weilin. In 1999 TIME's editors named this "unknown rebel" to its TIME 100 list of the century's most influential people. But as Pico Iyer noted in his profile, "… the heroes of the tank picture are two: the unknown figure who risked his life by standing in front of the juggernaut and the driver who rose to the moral challenge by refusing to mow down his compatriot."

CHINESE PROTESTER STOPS A COLUMN OF TANKS, 6/4/89
Stuart Franklin

RED OCTOBER

For much of 1993 Russia was a house divided, as Boris Yeltsin and his reform government vied for power with the parliament. Elected before the collapse of the Soviet Union in late 1991, the congress was filled with communists who viewed Yeltsin as a traitor. When Yeltsin announced he was disbanding the legislature, a rump group of angry Deputies occupied the building and threw up barricades to protect themselves—as seen in this picture by TIME's Anthony Suau.

On Oct. 3, thousands of anti-Yeltsin activists—a ragtag army of communists, neo-Nazis and just plain hooligans—converged on Moscow to support the Deputies. Marching through the city's broad avenues, the protesters unfurled hammer-and-sickle flags and called for the execution of leading reformers. The next day Yeltsin sent troops and tanks to open fire on the building, called the White House. The rebels were quashed, and Russia's reforms continued.

**HUTU MAN
WITH MACHETE
SCARS, 5/94**
James Nachtwey

THE MARK OF CAIN

In the spring and summer of 1994 two dramas of a very different nature played themselves out in Africa. The world celebrated with South Africans as voters there —including blacks casting their first ballots—named long-time political prisoner Nelson Mandela as their new President. But to the north, in Rwanda, a war between rival tribes, the Tutsi and the Hutu, reached genocidal proportions. As many as 1 million people were killed, while more than 2 million Hutu fled the country, taking refuge in camps later plagued by typhoid and cholera.

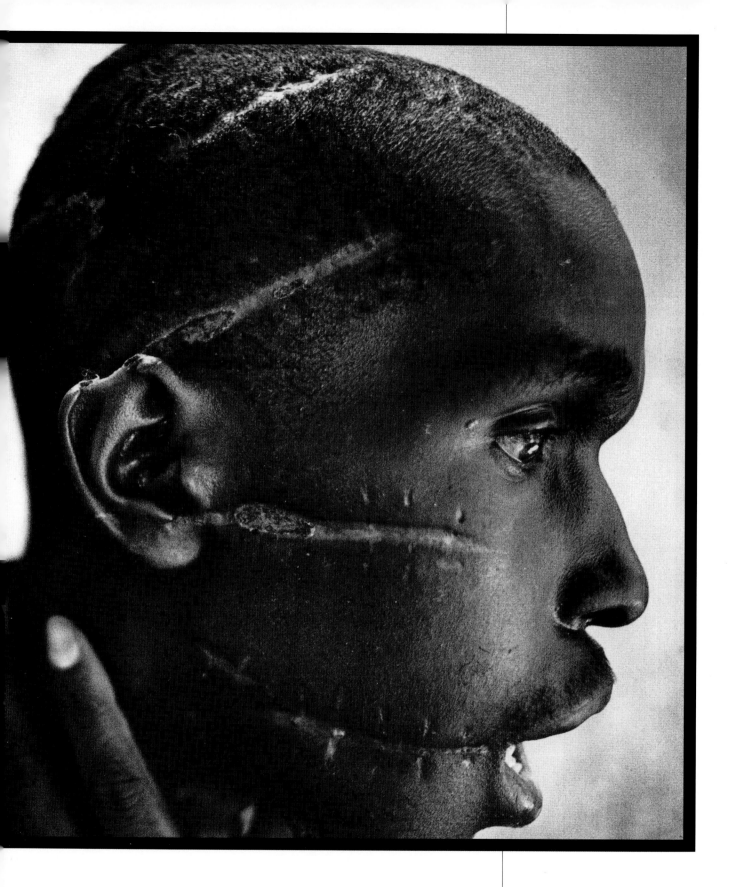

On assignment for TIME, photographer James Nachtwey took this portrait of a wealthy Hutu who bore the marks of the struggle on his face: suspected of sympathizing with the Tutsi, he was mutilated by the machetes of his fellow Hutu, members of the Interahamwe militia.

MEMENTO MORI

When a bomb destroyed the Alfred P. Murrah Federal Building in Oklahoma City in 1995, killing 168 people, the mass murder initially overwhelmed Americans but finally resolved itself into two images. The first was the twisted, skeletal ruins of the building itself. The second was a picture of fire fighter Chris Fields holding a tiny victim, one-year-old Baylee Almon, in his arms. However sad, the image inserted a necessary note of love and hope into a scenario devised by the terrorists as a rebuke to such feelings.

The picture was taken by amateur photographer Charles Porter, who was drawn by the explosion from his job at a nearby bank; it ran on front pages across America the next day. In its first report on the bombing, TIME noted how quickly the "image came to symbolize the tragedy." Porter received the Pulitzer Prize for news photography.

The baffling scene below is evidence of another tragedy: it is the sweater of a passenger on SwissAir Flight 111, which fell into the sea off the coast of Nova Scotia in September 1998. Flecked with the plane's debris, it is an appropriately cryptic memento of a crash that killed 229 but whose origin remains a mystery.

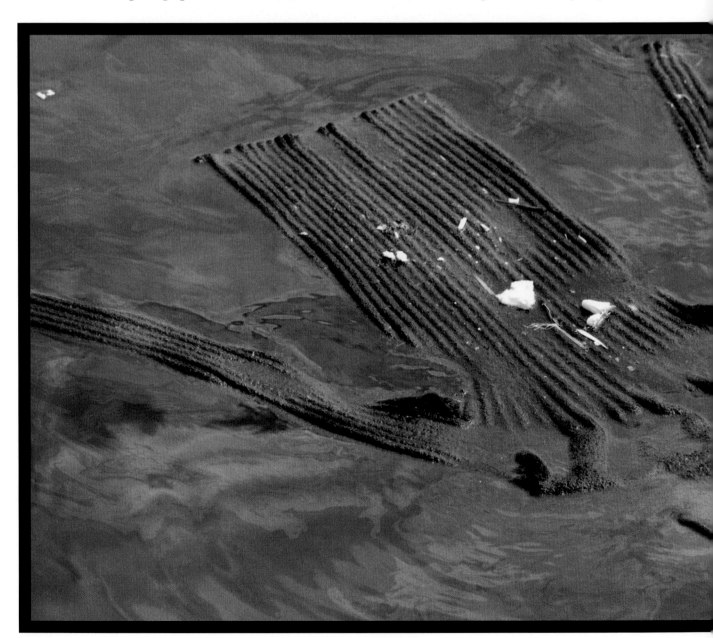

**FIRE FIGHTER AND
CHILD, OKLAHOMA
CITY, 4/19/95**
Charles H. Porter IV

**FLOTSAM FROM
AIRPLANE
CRASH, 9/98**
Sandor Fizli

**KOSOVAR
REFUGEES, 4/99**
Christopher Morris

FALSE DAWN

Throughout the 1990s Yugoslavia's President Slobodan Milosevic waged war against the non-Serb populations of his fragmented region under the grim banner of "ethnic cleansing." His campaign against the Muslim majority of Bosnia and Herzegovina was finally stopped by the Dayton peace accord of 1995. But then Milosevic turned his gaze south, to the Yugoslav province of Kosovo—land the Serbs hold dear as their ancestral home. But Kosovo's 2 million inhabitants were not Serbs: they were 90% ethnic Albanian Muslims.

In 1998 the province exploded as Kosovars demanded independence and sent guerrillas against the Yugoslav army. In March 1999, after Milosevic had spurned a NATO peace plan, allied planes began to bomb Yugoslavia. Milosevic quickly sent some 40,000 Serb troops—and ultranationalist gangs—rampaging through Kosovo. More than 800,000 Kosovars were routed from their homes; many of them fled to nearby Albania and Macedonia.

Veteran TIME photographer Christopher Morris took this picture of Kosovar refugees near the Macedonian border. Says TIME picture editor Michele Stephenson: "Chris took a lot of shots ... but he only filed one image. That was enough."

66A photograph is a secret about a secret. The more it tells you, the less you know.**99** — **DIANE ARBUS**

TO DOC

AN OASIS IN THE BADLANDS, 1905
Edward S. Curtis

UMENT

CHIEF RED HAWK of the once great Sioux tribe of the Plains sits astride a horse in the Badlands of the Dakotas. The photograph was taken in 1905 by Edward S. Curtis, who devoted his long career in photography to recording the lives of the remaining Indian tribes of North America. Curtis' intentions were quite clear: "These pictures were to be transcriptions for future generations that they might behold the Indian as nearly lifelike as possible." Here is the defining urge of the documentary photographer—to use the camera as a historian's instrument, preserving scenes that might otherwise vanish from our mind's eye.

Yet Curtis' picture is also a bit of a fake: Red Hawk wears full battle regalia, including a war bonnet—20 years after the last major battle of the Indian wars. The scene has been staged for the camera. Yet it remains a source of information that we might otherwise never have had—even as it packs an emotional wallop in its evocation of a vanishing world. The Indians cooperated with Curtis because, he claimed, "they have grasped the idea that this is to be a permanent memorial of their race, and it appeals to their imagination. A tribe that I have visited and studied lets another tribe know that after the present generation has passed away, men will know from this record what they were like, and what they did."

Throughout the century photographers have followed in Curtis' tracks, exploring, illuminating and preserving the days and ways of all kinds of cultures—from Sebastião Salgado's gold miners in Brazil to Weegee's flash-frozen New Yorkers to Diane Arbus' outcasts and freaks. In some cases the documentary photographer combines a historian's errand with an artist's eye. The result is an image that not only records the surface of things but also digs deeper to lay them bare, stripping them of social artifice to find truths that the façade conceals—an impulse expressed in the title of Weegee's collection of unblinking tabloid shots of the gritty streets of Manhattan, *Naked City*.

Documentary photographers straddle eras; their pictures are messages in bottles, bulletins that travel through time rather than space. As Lewis Hine said of the pictures he took of child laborers just after the turn of the century, "[Photographs are] the Human Document to keep the present and the future in touch with the past." ∎

TIME MACHINE

The photographer who took this scene is not known. The day he recorded, while not a typical one, was not so out-of-the-ordinary. Yet the picture stops us, for it seems able to take us directly into the presence of the past. It throbs with detail, tells a hundred stories. The signs in the store windows trace immigrants' dreams; the line of trolley cars powered by overhead lines reminds us that America was just toddling into the electrical age; the sea of millinery splendor invites a fashion lover's magnifying glass.

In its role as time machine, a picture's value appreciates

TO DOCUMENT

with age. This one offers much more information to us than it did to its contemporaries. They would have seen a fine picture of yesterday's celebration; we see a vanished world, fascinating in the very details that would have seemed humdrum to the people frozen in its frame.

MESSAGE IN A BOTTLE

Here is an image that speaks in a language we can no longer understand. It captures a China that seems closer to the time of Marco Polo than of Jiang Zemin, yet it was taken in 1914—after Picasso's Cubism, Einstein's relativity and Ford's flivver had pushed Europe and America into the modern age. The picture was taken by a Finnish priest, Hannu Haahti, who had been sent to China to act as a mediator in a dispute between different missionary groups. He took along a large wooden camera, with which he shot a number of

TO DOCUMENT

remarkable photos as a record of his journey. Seventy years later, the pictures were found in Finland, by pure coincidence, and were published for the first time. Here we see an interior scene—a store, it seems—in Mongtshisy. Haahti died in 1935, at age 68.

DESCENT INTO DARKNESS

Some pictures carry a special documentary burden: the scenes they show us must be preserved as proof of madness past. Above, German university students burn books at a 1933 rally. The event was reported in TIME's May 22, issue: "Undampened by a chilly drizzle, some 40,000 Germans jammed the square between Berlin's Friedrich Wilhelm University and the Opera House. Toward midnight a procession entered the square, headed by officers of the University's student dueling corps in their dress uniforms. Behind them came other students and a line of motor trucks piled high with books. More students clung to the trucks, waving flaring torches that they hurled through the air at the log pile. Blue flames of gasoline shot up, the pyre blazed. One squad of students formed a chain from the pyre to the trucks. Then came the books, passed from hand to hand … While the flames flared highest, up to a little flag-draped rostrum stumped club-footed, wild-eyed little Dr. Paul Joseph Goebbels, Minister of Propaganda and Public Enlightenment in the Nazi Cabinet, organizer of the great midnight bibliocaust. 'Jewish intellectualism is dead!' cried he. 'The German folk soul can again express itself.' All over Germany similar pyres blazed with similar books."

The original notes on the back of the picture at right read, "[German] schoolchildren do not pour out of schools at the end of the day, whooping and rejoicing at being set free, but march out in military formation."

GERMAN SCHOOLBOYS SALUTE, DATE UNKNOWN
Photographer Unknown

UNFLINCHING EYES

In the 1930s and '40s, Arthur Fellig (1899-1968) sat atop the heap of New York City's scrambling tabloid photographers. He reveled in the moniker he was awarded by his envious rivals—"Weegee"—a play on the board game Ouija, for Fellig often sniffed out crime scenes before his peers did. With tabloid gusto he embellished his handle, stamping his pictures WEEGEE THE FAMOUS.

Fellig not only got a head start on his foes, he also beat them to the finish line, using a miniature darkroom in the trunk of his car to develop the scenes he shot through his Speed Graphic camera—scenes that often featured a gruesome car crash or crime and the giddy rubbernecking it unleashed. In *The Critic*,

Weegee pinned down a different kind of crash—a collision of cultures as a street person confronts two social butterflies at the Metropolitan Opera. But this time he cheated, staging the shot by plying a Bowery derelict with wine and placing her in smarm's way.

Diane Arbus (1923-71) is often regarded primarily as an "art" photographer, but that designation overlooks the extent to which her compelling, direct portraits are works of journalism, reports from front lines that many of us normally avoid. Often photographing subjects who were social outcasts for one reason or another—whose very otherness made them "aristocrats" in her eyes—Arbus left behind a body of great documentary pictures.

Left:

THE CRITIC, 11/22/43
Arthur Fellig ("Weegee")

**BOY WITH A STRAW HAT WAITING TO
MARCH IN A PRO-WAR PARADE, 1967**
Diane Arbus

EASTER SUNDAY IN CHICAGO, 1941
Russell Lee

COOL CATS

Old pictures are a sociologist's dream: in these two photos we find traces of the changing fabric of mid-century America.

The picture at left records a scandal in bohemia: when Beats in Greenwich Village decided to name Miss Beatnik 1959—dare we suspect the contest was a put-on?—the crown went to a ringer, a bathing-suited, uptown chorus girl. The outcast "square," though surrounded by Beats, might as well be miles away. But today our eyes are more interested in the details newspaper photographer Nat Fein recorded about the Beats: their haircuts, their beards, their rather staid chinos—and, most of all, the casual ease with which blacks and whites get along; they are flaunting their freedom from racism for Fein's camera.

The Beats' diversity reflects the changing population of the nation's cities, as African Americans moved upriver from Southern farms to Northern streets. An unknown photographer's picture of a group of self-assured, stylish black boys on Easter Sunday morning in Chicago is a study in urban cool.

TO DOCUMENT

**KU KLUX KLAN RALLY,
NORTH CAROLINA, 7/65**
Charles Moore

Below:
**MISSISSIPPI FARMERS,
7/63**
Charles Moore

INSIDE THE KLAN

Sometimes the most challenging aspect of documenting a scene is getting access to it. How did a photographer on assignment for LIFE get inside a large Ku Klux Klan rally? Asked to recall the events of that evening for this book, Charles Moore said, "I was invited by the local Grand Dragon, who was eager to get publicity for the Klan. It was a major gathering; there was a big crowd of locals, and the national Imperial Wizard was there. But when some Klan

members saw me taking pictures, they started to threaten me. It got pretty hairy. I went to the Grand Dragon and said, 'I don't think you want the kind of publicity you'll get if your guys kill a LIFE photographer.' So he assigned two of his bully boys with clubs to be my escorts." The woman in the foreground, Moore said, is the Grand Wizard's wife.

Moore, a native of Alabama, took historic news shots of violent racial confrontations in the South (*see page 86*); he also recorded the context within which they occurred. The scene at left, a black and white farmer chatting in rural Mississippi during the tense summer of 1963, captures the complex interplay between the races in the South: for decades a genuine sort of amity reigned— as long as the "Jim Crow" laws of segregation were strictly understood and observed by all concerned.

BLACK, WHITE AND GOLD

For many people, the scene at left takes a moment to sink in: at first glance, it might be a still taken from a Nature Channel documentary on the industrious carpenter ant. But as we absorb the picture, we realize we are looking at human beings engaged in a great labor: Sebastião Salgado's photo is of a modern-day gold rush in Brazil.

The story of Brazil's gold fever echoes that of America's fabled Forty-Niners. In 1980 a cowhand discovered a gold nugget in a stream in the state of Para in Brazil; within two weeks 10,000 gold diggers, or *garimperos,* had arrived on the site. When Salgado shot the scene in 1986, 50,000 men were laboring in the man-made hole; the "mudhogs" scale slippery ladders while carrying heavy sacks of soil for sifting. The black-and-white film turns the scene into a study in massed forms reminiscent of a Gustave Doré engraving.

Salgado traveled the world for six years to record scenes of manual labor for his book, *Workers: An Archaeology of the Industrial Age.* His urge, the photographer says, was to document skills—and panoramas like this one— that may soon vanish as new technologies make them obsolete.

Both Photos:
**GOLD MINERS
IN BRAZIL, 1986**
Sebastião Salgado

When TIME'S editors need pictures that record the everyday life of modern Americans, photographer Steve Liss is likely to get the call. His pictures make up a patchwork quilt of our national life, ranging from Arbus-like portraits of ordinary citizens in their homes to emblematic glimpses of the stuff we look at repeatedly without really seeing: neon motel signs, old-timers in love, kids at play.

If we compare this picture to the photograph of the Labor Day celebration in Buffalo, N.Y., at the beginning of this chapter, we see how Americans' definitions of the good life have changed over the course of the century. In the early 1900s, as more and more young people left the farmstead for the city, there was an electric attraction to the clotted, bustling streets of the metropolis: "Take me out to the ball game/ Take me out to the crowd." But at century's end, when most Americans live in cities or suburbs, the ideal is just the opposite. Now the goal is to "get away from it all" by packing the immediate family and a Coleman lantern into a recreational vehicle and heading out of town for the wide-open spaces—far from the madding crowd.

TRAILER-PARK PICNIC IN UTAH, 1997
Steve Liss

TO CAPTURE

THE CAMERA'S eye stops time, offering indelible records of events that our eyes may have beheld but that unfolded too rapidly for us to absorb. Within this unique instant, even as original prints yellow with age, pictures live in an eternal present, and their captions are written in the present tense.

Thanks to technological improvements in the century's first decades, bulky box cameras and long exposure times gave way to small, portable cameras that pared time into cross-sections. A new kind of photojournalism emerged: pictures that showed the exact instant of a news event, even catching death in the act. Soon, scenes that once would have been witnessed by only a few eyes were seen by millions in newspapers and magazines: the electrocution of a murderer, the point-blank execution of a suspected Viet Cong agent, even the assassination of a President. Like the picture at right, the murder of Lee Harvey Oswald by Jack Ruby, such historic images have turned out to be among the most memorable of the century, the icons that make up the visual map of our times.

For photographers, pursuing singular moments like these demands courage and quick reflexes—and capturing them takes a toll on the spirit. In 1994, for instance, the world's media were flooded with images from South Africa: two white, neo-Nazi militiamen, wounded in a gun battle with black troops in the black homeland of Bophuthatswana, were executed in front of a crowd of stunned photojournalists. TIME later interviewed several of the photographers. One, Kevin Carter, berated himself: "I made the mistake of running for cover instead of turning around, coldly analyzing the situation and shooting a great execution picture." In those final three words we catch the slippery morality of this process: How can a cold-blooded execution be great? Another cameraman, Gideon Mendel, elaborated, "Photographers are aware that violence is a valuable commodity. When I heard that some of the photographers had been at the execution [he missed it and shot the aftermath], I said, 'F___, I missed the event.' That's a rather peculiar thing for a human being to say: 'Damn, I wasn't at the scene of a killing.' I am disturbed at seeing hordes of photographers chasing after violence, although I am a part of it." Like Mendel, we may be disturbed by such images—yet we cannot look away. ■

"Inside, a voice is screaming, 'My God!'

But it is time to work. Deal with the rest later."

— KEVIN CARTER

JACK RUBY SHOOTS LEE HARVEY OSWALD, 11/24/63
Bob Jackson

**EXECUTION OF RUTH
SNYDER, 1/12/28**
Thomas Howard

CRASH OF THE *HINDENBURG*, 5/6/37
Murray Becker

SINGULAR SENSATIONS

In the heyday of the image-driven tabloid newspaper, editors and photographers frantically vied for scoops. The pursuit of sensation reached its zenith on Jan. 13, 1928, when the New York *Daily News*—whose logo sported a camera and the blurb "New York's Picture Newspaper"—ran a front-page photo of the electrocution in Sing Sing prison of Ruth Snyder, a convicted killer. The image was taken with a modified miniature camera strapped to Thomas Howard's ankle. The headline: DEAD!

Nine years later, the crash of the German zeppelin *Hindenburg* became, in TIME's words, "the most completely witnessed disaster in the history of commercial aviation." The tragedy that killed 36 people was broadcast live on radio and was recorded on newsreel footage and in a number of still photos, including this memorable image by Murray Becker.

SUICIDE, 1942
I. Russell Sorgi

Right:
FALL OF A FLYING WALLENDA, 2/1/62
O.C. Hansen

TO CAPTURE

SUSPENSION OF DISBELIEF

Hostages to gravity, two young women are caught in free flight. The lens turns their falls—a blur and an intake of breath to spectators—into still lifes we can ponder.

In the picture above, a woman reported to be stricken by a divorce hurls herself to her death at a hotel in Buffalo, N.Y. When the woman's intention to jump became clear, the photographer stationed himself to record her eight-story fall; a policeman at the door holds back a curious crowd.

At right, 17-year-old aerialist Jana Schepp jumps into an improvised net after her brother and cousin, members of the Flying Wallendas, fell to their deaths when their signature no-net high-wire act went awry.

HIROSHIMA, GROUND ZERO

Here is a photograph taken 10 minutes after the world changed forever. It captures not only an instant in time but also the dawn of an era—the atomic age—with the explosion of the first atom bomb over Hiroshima, Japan. As TIME reported, "The single bomb … almost completely wiped out everything within 4.4 square miles, killed 70,000 to 80,000 people. Some 62,000 of the 90,000 buildings in the urban area were leveled." Japanese photographer Yoshito Matsushige's image is one of very few to record the impact of the bomb just after detonation.

James Agee's story in TIME caught the unease of the moment. "With the controlled splitting of the atom, humanity, already profoundly perplexed and disunified, was brought inescapably into a new age in which all thoughts and things were split— and far from controlled. The sudden achievement of victory was a mercy to the Japanese no less than to the United Nations; but mercy born of a ruthless force beyond anything in human chronicle … The race had been won, but the demonstration of power against living creatures instead of dead matter created a bottomless wound in the living conscience of the race."

TO CAPTURE

HIROSHIMA TEN MINUTES AFTER THE BOMBING, 8/6/45
Yoshito Matsushige

**THE ASSASSINATION
OF JOHN F. KENNEDY,
11/22/63**
Abraham Zapruder

TO CAPTURE

DEATH IN THE AFTERNOON

One of the most historic series of images of the century was
not recorded by a professional photojournalist, but by an
amateur home-movie maker, Dallas dress manufacturer
Abraham Zapruder. Stationed near his office along the
route of a motorcade carrying President John Kennedy and

wife Jacqueline, Zapruder, a Kennedy admirer, recorded the shooting of the President on his 8-mm. camera. This is frame No. 246 of the film, enlarged many times.

Landing in Dallas hours after the event, LIFE magazine Pacific Coast editor Richard Stolley was tipped off to the film; he reached Zapruder and bought the rights to it the next morning. Time Inc. paid Zapruder $150,000; he immediately donated $25,000 of the money to the widow of Dallas police officer J.D. Tippett, who had been slain by Lee Harvey Oswald shortly after the assassination.

SHOTS SEEN ROUND THE WORLD

The long struggle in Vietnam yielded many memorable photographs; here are two of them. Above, Eddie Adams' picture shows General Nguyen Ngoc Loan, chief of the South Vietnam police, executing a suspected Vietcong officer at point-blank range on a Saigon street during the 1968 Tet Offensive. The victim's helplessness and the brutal efficiency of his killer caught in a single image many of the elements that were turning a majority of Americans against the war. The photo won the Pulitzer Prize in 1969.

At right, Buddhist monk Quang Duc stoically bears self-immolation in a photo by Malcolm Browne, an AP reporter. The monk was protesting religious oppression by South Vietnam's Diem regime. The image, one of the first to alert Americans to the passions roiling the region, was controversial. TIME printed it, but some other publications did not.

**EXECUTION IN A
SAIGON STREET,
2/1/68**
Eddie Adams

Below:
**QUANG DUC
IMMOLATES
HIMSELF, 6/11/63**
Malcolm Browne

TO CAPTURE

TO CAPTURE

CLINGING TO LIFE

This picture, sad enough in itself, becomes far sadder when its full story is told. In 1985 the eruption of the Nevado del Ruíz volcano in Colombia hurled waves of mud and debris down the slopes of the mountain; entire villages were buried and some 25,000 people died. Omayra Sanchez was trapped in the muck; rescue workers tried to extricate her but failed, and the young girl died after this picture was taken.

The tragic ending to the story illuminates the slippery moral dilemmas of photojournalism. Frank Fournier was simply recording a girl in peril; he could not know the outcome of the situation. Had she survived, he might have been hailed for catching a moment of high tension, but when the rescue attempts failed, the image changed— and to some it may seem an unnecessary exploitation of the girl's suffering.

Complicating the dilemma is this central fact: for once, we are not simply looking at a picture; this time, the picture is looking back. Revelation or exploitation? The answer must lie in the eye of the beholder, staring into the eyes of the girl.

**GIRL TRAPPED IN
MUDSLIDE, 11/16/85**
Frank Fournier

**STREET BATTLE IN
NORTHERN IRELAND,
1981**
James Nachtwey

TIME OF TROUBLES

Since 1969 the six provinces of Ireland that remain under British sovereignty have been plagued by "the Troubles," a civil war of terrorism that pitted Loyalist Protestants against independence-seeking Catholics and claimed as many as 3,500 lives. An accord reached on Good Friday, 1998, may bring peace to the region.

This picture was taken after a group of Catholic demonstrators in Belfast had hijacked a car, parked it in the entranceway to a British barracks and set it on fire. When the British dispatched an armored vehicle to remove the flaming barricade, the protesters respond by hurling gas bombs at the massive machine.

CARGO OF TEARS

The explosion of the space shuttle *Challenger* is one of those few events—like the bombing of Pearl Harbor and the assassination of John F. Kennedy—that arrives with such forceful surprise that most Americans who were alive at the time can still remember exactly where they were when they first heard the news.

The tragedy of the *Challenger* came after space travel had seemed to lose its element of risk—largely due to the shuttle's frequent flights. Even worse, *Challenger* was carrying the first U.S. civilian to travel into space, schoolteacher Christa McAuliffe, under a heavily promoted NASA program intended to make space flight seem more approachable to the common person.

When we step back from this image, which is branded so deeply in many minds, we realize it is visually almost abstract, a scrawl of smoke against the sky. It is the terrible knowledge we bring to the picture that freights it with sorrow.

THE *CHALLENGER* EXPLODES, 1/28/86
Bruce Weaver

ERUPTION OF
MOUNT PINATUBO,
6/17/91
Alberto Garcia

TO CAPTURE

ON THE RUN

When the Mount Pinatubo volcano in the Philippines—dormant for 611 years—erupted in 1991, it was accompanied by earthquakes and torrential rains that took 330 lives.

Photographers raced to the scene—and some ended up racing *from* the scene, as the volcano sent a gigantic cloud of smoke, ash and gas rolling across their escape route.

Traveling ahead of his colleagues, Alberto Garcia stopped and caught this potent reminder of the relative power of man vs. volcano. The story had a happy ending: the photographers (and their pictures) survived.

**WEEPING SERGEANT
IN GULF WAR, 2/28/91**
David C. Turnley

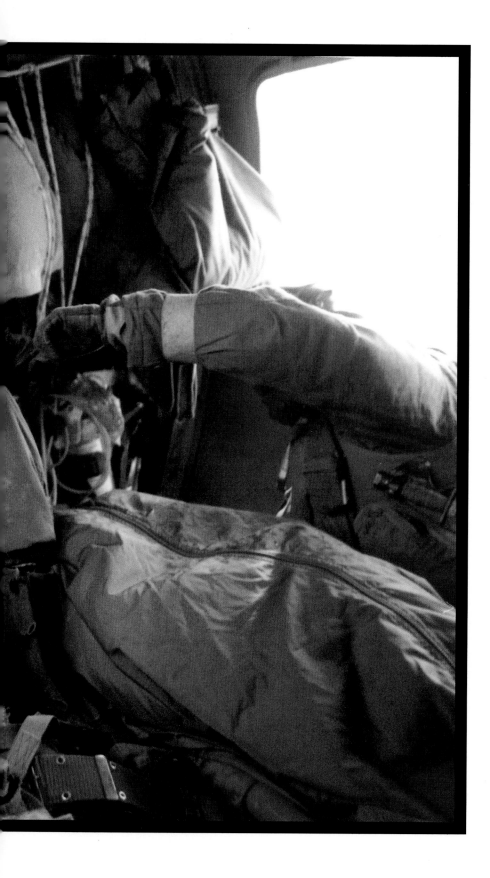

The 1991 Gulf War that pitted a U.S.-led allied coalition against Iraqi strongman Saddam Hussein was a new kind of battle for Americans: it was both the first major war following the demise of the Soviet Union and the first high-tech war. With much of the fighting conducted by unmanned missiles and laser-guided bombs—and with the Pentagon tightly controlling access to the front after the ground war began— the war did not produce the strong images that linger in the national consciousness and define World War II and the long struggle in Vietnam.

This picture, which shows the aftermath of a battle rather than the battle itself, is one of the most memorable from the Gulf War. David Turnley captured U.S. Sergeant Ken Kozakiewicz, who was being evacuated from the front in a medical helicopter, at the moment when he learned that the corpse in the body bag to his left is that of a fellow tank crewman who was killed by "friendly fire."

Said Kozakiewicz's father on seeing this picture: "I saw the look on my boy's face, and I know he will never be the same."

"**HOW ABOUT** some good news for a change?" This frequently heard lament echoes a dilemma as old as journalism itself, one that reverses an old saw—because, for photographers, good news is often no news. Imagine you're shooting pictures for a small-town newspaper. Which story would you prefer to cover: HOUSE BURNS DOWN—FIVE LEFT HOMELESS or MAYOR SAYS CRIME IS DOWN? It's no contest: Where's the fire?

Now and then a gifted individual manages to capture the spirit of joy in an image so strong it speaks to all of us—like Ralph Crane's exhilarating picture of hot rodders playing "chicken" at 70 m.p.h. ("Surprisingly, some of this generation of young Californians survived," commented Crane.) And some historic events have produced wonderful photos, as the following pages show. But all too often, good news on the grand scale arrives prepackaged. When it's time to put on a bicentennial blowout, a Fourth of July parade or a rededication of the Statue of Liberty, party planners strive for photo-ops on steroids. They order up fireworks by the case, balloons by the gross, singers and dancers by the hundreds, confetti by the ... well, in large quantities. But what party planners can't order up is precisely what we want from a picture: spontaneity, surprise, insight. Is it any wonder that the result of all their staging is a photo that looks staged?

There's a deeper force at work here: crime and punishment are far more intriguing than law and order. Dante knew it: his *Inferno* is still widely read, while only scholars seem to get through *Il Paradiso*. Milton knew it: Lucifer is by far the most interesting character in *Paradise Lost*. Hollywood knows it: we'll spare you an example. And your local nightly TV news team knows it; the story hierarchy is brutally simple: "It if bleeds, it leads." Like it or not, the media will continue to bring bad news into our homes. And we'll continue to demand that the messenger be shot—after we've digested the pictures. In the meantime, let's take a moment to celebrate. ∎

JOYRIDERS PLAYING "CHICKEN," 1949
Ralph Crane

T E "I think there's some sense of magic in the fact that what's out there can be caught in this little box." – JOHN LOENGARD

**THE LIBERATION
OF PARIS, 8/12/44**
Robert Capa

VIVE LA FRANCE!

The liberation of Paris after four years of Nazi rule was a grand moment—so grand that TIME's constitutionally moderate editors seem to have broken out the bubbly as they wrote the introduction to the magazine's eyewitness account of the celebration: "It was one of the great days of all time. For Paris is the city of all free mankind, and its liberation last week was one of the great events of all time." Translation: Let the good times roll!

TIME boasted that its chief war correspondent, Charles Christian Wertenbaker, was the first U.S. newsman to enter the city. He was traveling with celebrated LIFE photographer Robert Capa; their jeep directly followed the armored car of General Jacques Leclerc as Free French forces entered the city through the Porte d'Orléans.

Wertenbaker's report: "I have seen the faces of young people in love and the faces of old people at peace with their God. I have never seen in any face such joy as radiated from the faces of the people of Paris this morning. This is no day for restraint, and I could not write with restraint if I wanted to. Your correspondent and your photographer Bob Capa drove into Paris with eyes that would not stay dry, and we were no more ashamed of it than were the people who wept as they embraced us. The people … waved arms and flags and flowers; they climbed aboard the cars and jeeps embracing the French and us alike; they uttered a great mass cry of delight that swelled and died down and swelled to a greater height. They cried: *'Vive De Gaulle!'* and *'Vive Leclerc!'* But one word repeated over and over rose above all other words. It was: *Merci! Merci! Merci!"*

TIMES SQUARE, V-J DAY, 8/15/45
Alfred Eisenstaedt

EXIT STRATEGIES

The last months of World War II—which TIME once called "the last good war"—produced two pictures that are among the most memorable of the century. Veteran LIFE photographer Alfred Eisenstaedt tells the story of the famous picture at left in his book, *Eisenstaedt on Eisenstaedt* (Abbeville Press; 1985): "In Times Square on V-J day I saw a sailor running along the street grabbing any and every girl in sight. Whether she was a grandmother, stout, thin, old, didn't make any difference. I was running ahead of him with my Leica looking back over my shoulder. But none of the pictures that were possible pleased me. Then suddenly, in a flash, I saw something white being grabbed. I turned around and clicked the moment the sailor kissed the nurse."

Six months earlier, the A.P.'s Joe Rosenthal had captured one of the moments that made V-J day possible: the U.S. victory on Japanese-held Iwo Jima. As Rosenthal climbed up Mount Suribachi, just taken by Marines, he learned they had raised a flag at the peak. He arrived just in time to catch five more Marines as they raised a larger, 4-ft. by 8-ft. flag in its place. The sculptural quality of the result was pure, glorious accident.

FLAG RAISING ON IWO JIMA, 2/23/45
Joe Rosenthal

SUBLIME VISIONS

Ansel Adams (1902-84) is the only photographer to appear on the cover of TIME. In that 1979 story, TIME art critic Robert Hughes noted that the celebrated portraitist of America's vast natural panoramas had no use for the photojournalism of advocacy. Among colleagues, says Hughes, Adams earned "a reputation as the least socially committed of serious American photographers." But while Adams may have refused to deal with the standard subjects of many Depression-era photographers—the breadlines, the rallies, the bums—his photographs played a formative role in the environmental movement. Adams spent 60 years working with the Sierra Club, 37 of them on its board of directors—not bad for one who called advocacy in photojournalism "propaganda."

Nor was Adams a documentary photojournalist in the traditional sense. As Hughes points out, "The landscapes on which his reputation rests are scarcely concerned with documentation at all. There are no people in them. They say nothing about society or history. They contain no news." But while Adams' pictures are beautiful as purely aesthetic objects—he took enormous pains in reproducing them—they certainly have brought the "news" of the West's grandeur to millions.

Pleas for conservation? A new photojournalism of nature? Or simply sublime studies in light and shade? However we approach Adams' work, it shines with a celebratory spirit: in Hughes' words, the "sense of a miraculous, beneficent clarity, of vision ecstatically distributed between the near and the far."

CLEARING WINTER STORM, YOSEMITE NATIONAL PARK, 1944
Ansel Adams

**BRIDAL COUPLE
IN BEIRUT, 1983**
Jay Ullal

TO CELEBRATE

JUST LIKE ROMEO AND JULIET

"Two households, both alike in dignity,/ In fair Beirut, where we lay our scene …" Well, we've taken liberties with Shakespeare's text, but this scene from Lebanon's rubble-strewn capital certainly proves that love can still sprout amid ancient grudges—and modern ruins.

The bride is Christian, the groom is Muslim, and the setting is the infamous "green line" that split Beirut down the middle in the stormy 1980s.

Lebanon's civil war lasted from 1975 to 1990 and claimed some 150,000 victims—including 241 U.S. Marines, killed in a 1983 terrorist bombing. Though now at peace, Lebanon remains divided among three main groups—Maronite Catholics and Sunni and Shi'ite Muslims—while its political reins are still firmly held by Syria's President Hafez Assad.

GATHERING OF THE TRIBES

When it's time to celebrate, cultures around the world turn to music and dance. The photograph on the right shows one such moment: it was taken in Zaïre, where photographer José Azel captured costumed and painted Pygmies of the Efe tribe celebrating a coming-of-age ritual, a young woman's entry into puberty as she begins to menstruate. Among the Efe people, such occasions are observed by a ritual sequestering of the young woman, followed by dancing and feasting. Pygmies are one of the world's largest remaining populations of hunter-gatherers; some 150,000 of them range across seven African countries, generally living in a symbiotic relationship with more settled farming tribes.

Far across the globe, as the photograph below shows, the people may be larger, but the instincts are not so different: let's strip down, get with the rhythm and dance—and if the mosh pit turns into a mud pit, well, here's mud in your eye. You don't have to be a cultural anthropologist to figure out that underneath the muck, these young revelers, like the Pygmies, are probably feeling pretty good about their sexuality. The scene is the Woodstock II festival in 1994, held 25 years after the original counterculture music and arts fair.

Yet while some of the impulses in the two photos may be similar, the differences are telling. As TIME music critic Christopher John Farley pointed out, the most naked aspect of Woodstock II was its capitalism. Its Eco-Village, billed as educating the public about the environment, resembled a strip mall where you could buy clothes, camping gear and even Woodstock air ($2 a bottle). In the First World, it seems, the cost of getting primitive just keeps going up.

WOODSTOCK II FESTIVAL, 8/94
Peter Essick

CEREMONIAL DANCE, ZAIRE, 1987
José Azel

DIVING INTO THE RIVER OF COLOR

Photographer Raghubir Singh spent his career celebrating the many-hued tapestry of life in his native India—like these young men in Benares, who are diving into the sacred Ganges from a temple half-submerged by monsoon floods. As Singh wrote in the introduction to his book *River of* *Color* (Phaidon Press; 1998): "Unlike those in the West, Indians have always intuitively seen and controlled color … the Indian photographer cannot produce the angst and alienation rooted in the works of Western photographers." Instead, Singh embraced everyday life with his camera,

capturing it in a palette of translucent splendor. In April 1999, after his work for TIME, the New York *Times* and *National Geographic* had won acclaim, and even as a retrospective of his pictures was showing at the Art Institute of Chicago, Singh suffered a heart attack and died at 58.

TEMPLE DIVERS IN BENARES, 1987
Raghubir Singh

TO CELEBRATE

**PRO-DEMOCRACY PROTESTER
IN TIANANMEN SQUARE, 5/89**
Stuart Franklin

Right:
**SMASHING THE BERLIN WALL,
11/9/89**
Anthony Suau

PEOPLE POWER

The year 1989 was one of those rare times when the tectonic plates of history shift beneath our feet, and nothing after is ever quite the same. In Germany the result was joyful, as a hated wall came tumbling down. In China the result was tragic, as a massive protest in Beijing was squelched by army tanks.

The Berlin Wall was perhaps the single most tangible symbol of the cold war. Built in August 1961, for 28 years it had stood as a symbol of the division of Europe and the world, of communist suppression, of the xenophobia of a regime that had to lock its people in lest they be tempted by another, freer life. But at midnight on Nov. 9, the 28-mile-long scar through the heart of a once proud European capital—and the soul of a people—began to crumble. When the teetering East German government announced it would open the wall, impatient, festive citizens took matters into their own hands, bringing out hammers and chisels and braving water cannons to whack away at the grim symbol of imprisonment.

Earlier that year a hunger strike by 3,000 Chinese students in Tiananmen Square had swelled into a riotous bloom of people power, as protesters created a mini-city devoted to freedom. For a few brief weeks, a sense of exuberant possibility captivated the pro-democracy protesters. But on June 4, the brief flame of joy was extinguished in a government massacre. The exact number of deaths has never been determined.

FIFTIETH ANNIVERSARY OF D-DAY, 6/6/94
David Burnett

HAPPY WARRIOR

The day was June 6, 1994—the 50th anniversary of D-day, the Allied invasion of German-occupied Normandy that historian Stephen Ambrose called "the greatest event of this century." Bob Williams, a veteran of the battle, was one of 40 former paratroopers who took part in a commemorative jump. He had just completed his drop when David Burnett took this photo; Williams was moving quickly to avoid being hit by some 600 other parachutists who were landing around him.

Said TIME's Hugh Sidey of this last great cantonment of D-day veterans: "There was a beautiful sadness about the moment. The serenity of the thin crescent of beach as it lies today was seen by those on excursion boats in the English Channel and by President Bill Clinton at dawn from the deck of the U.S. aircraft carrier *George Washington.* More than one water-borne spectator sensed how fragile the whole D-day operation must have been, successful finally by its audacity and the spirits of young servicemen sustained by the singular strength that comes from freedom … More than he realized, Bill Clinton may have typified a younger generation's response to this intense lesson from another world, another war. It was as if he had long been an indifferent son, blanking out for decades a nation's old war stories, then waking suddenly to the heroics of a dim past and wanting to go back to nurture the memories and understand them better."

❝Photography is a small voice, at best, but sometimes one photograph … can lure our senses to awareness.**❞**

—W. EUGENE SMITH

TO **AD**

VOCATE

SEGREGATED WATER FOUNTAIN, 1950
Elliott Erwitt

PICTURES MAY have a small voice, but they work in ways that bypass speech. Perhaps our optical nerves are wired to our brains through our hearts, for images first touch us, then persuade us. So Elliott Erwitt's image of a black man at a water fountain in North Carolina in 1950 not only records the brutishness of life under segregation, it is also a powerful argument against it.

Jacob Riis was the first American to put his camera to work as a tool of persuasion. His devastating portraits of urban poverty in the 1890s inspired reform groups to hire photographers to document the social conditions they deplored. Lewis Hine's pictures of young workers were paid for by the National Child Labor Committee, and New Dealers calling for federal aid to people mired in the Depression dispatched a corps of photographers to record their plight. In the 1980s the Domestic Abuse Awareness Project funded the work of Donna Ferrato, whose pictures of violence in the home focused attention on previously hidden crimes.

By the 1960s, the realization that pictures aroused passions had moved to the other side of the lens. Interest groups learned that by manipulating authorities into harsh reactions, they could create visual epiphanies, scenes that manifested injustice for all to see. Suddenly, photographs that advocated an end to segregation were not the quiet but pointed essays of Erwitt; they were the highly charged news shots of Charles Moore, showing police turning dogs and water cannons against black demonstrators. A few years later, protesters at the 1968 Democratic Convention taunted Chicago's head-busting police with a phrase that showed how well the lesson of visual politics had been learned: "The whole world is watching." ■

SATANIC MILLS

At the turn of the century, the camera became one of the most powerful tools of the burgeoning reform movement. Jacob Riis' book *How the Other Half Lives* (1890) had forced Americans to confront the squalor of the nation's slums, and it inspired other photographers to document the plight of immigrants and the underclass.

Sociologist Lewis Hine (1874-1940) had been taking pictures of immigrants arriving at New York City's Ellis Island as research. In 1908 he went to work as a cameraman for the National Child Labor Committee, a group that was pushing for reform of the nation's labor laws. Said Hine: "In the early days of my child-labor activities I was an investigator with a camera attachment … but the emphasis became reversed until the camera stole the whole show."

Hine traveled America recording the shocking youth of many factory hands; the NCLC used his pictures in its long campaign to pass laws forbidding the employment of children. Here, two boys work a cotton mill—but they are so dwarfed by the machine, perhaps we should say *it* is working them.

TO ADVOCATE

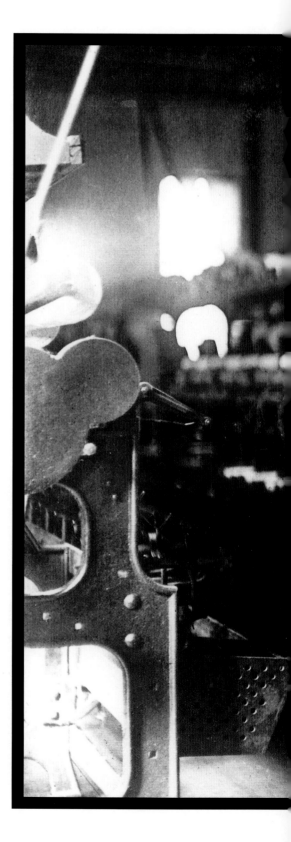

DOWN AND OUT

Franklin D. Roosevelt's New Deal swept across America during the hard times of the 1930s, sparking a renaissance of social concern. Aware of the power of photos to rally public opinion, New Dealers created the Farm Security Administration photography project to document the harsh conditions that beset rural Americans. The FSA, headed by the energetic Roy Stryker, hired some of the country's finest photojournalists—including Dorothea Lange, Walker Evans and Ben Shahn—to travel the nation and record the struggles of farmers and "Okies," hobos and tramps. Between 1935 and 1943, FSA cameras took some 270,000 photos, putting an indelible human face on an economic tragedy.

Lange's picture of a migrant mother in California has become an icon; though it is a portrait and presents little sociological detail, the woman's eyes tell us all we need to know of the Dust Bowl and the Depression. The woman might be 50; when Lange asked her age, it turned out to be 32. She was the mother of seven children.

The problem was nationwide: across the country in Florida, an FSA photographer found workers living in similar conditions, below.

TO **ADVOCATE**

WORKERS CAMP IN FLORIDA, 1939
Photographer Unknown, Farm Security Administration

MIGRANT MOTHER, 3/36
Dorothea Lange

THE DOGS OF WAR

In the 1960s, photographs played a key role in the struggle that earned black Americans an equal place in U.S. society, as civil rights leaders learned that forcing confrontations with the authorities created images that moved minds.

In the spring of 1963, protesters led by Martin Luther King Jr. exposed the cruelty of the police of Birmingham, Ala. ("the citadel of blind, die-hard segregation," in TIME's words). Training water cannons on some blacks and turning attack dogs against others, police under "Bull" Connor became King's unwitting allies. In 1964, one year after it ran the Birmingham pictures of Charles Moore and others, TIME said, "The Negroes had created their crisis—and Connor had made it a success … Because of Connor, the riots seared the front pages of the world press, outraged millions of people."

TO ADVOCATE

POLICE DOGS ATTACK DEMONSTRATOR IN BIRMINGHAM, 5/4/63
Charles Moore

MOTHER BATHES VICTIM OF MERCURY POLLUTION, 1971
W. Eugene Smith

POISON'S PRICE

W. Eugene Smith (1918-1978) was one of the century's great photojournalists, a complex man who brought a rare sensitivity to subjects ranging from war to personal portraits to social issues like environmental pollution. In 1971 Smith journeyed to Japan, where he recorded the impact of industrial pollution on the citizens of a small fishing village, Minimata. Here Tomoko Uemura, 15, born deformed because of mercury poisoning,, is given a special bath by her mother

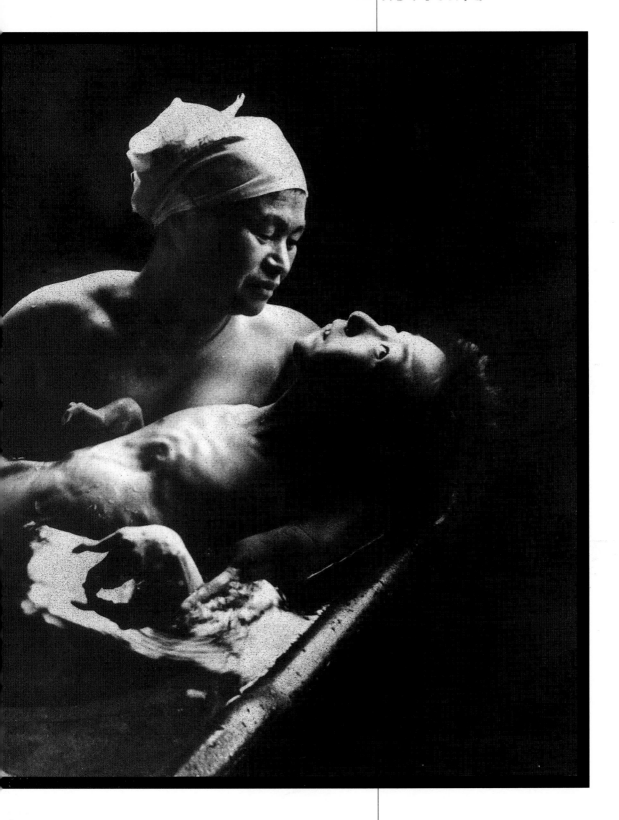

to relieve her symptoms. Weeks after he shot this
picture, Smith was beaten by company goons.
Uemura died six years later, but Smith's pictures
helped the victims finally win a settlement
from the corporation behind the pollution.

REPORTS FROM THE FRONT

The crusading impulse that animated the work of Lewis Hine, Dorothea Lange and other activist photographers continues to inspire contemporary photojournalists. Donna Ferrato spent more than a decade chronicling the horrors of family violence for the Domestic Abuse Awareness Project. Among the scenes she captured was the one below: an eight-year-old boy admonishing his father, who was being arrested for abusing the child's mother. "I hate you! Never come back to my house!" the boy screamed. Moments before, he had called the police when the father began to beat his wife and threaten her with a knife.

Eugene Richards spent years capturing a reality that many prefer to avoid: the wages of drug abuse and the crime it creates. At the height of the crack-cocaine epidemic that first struck U.S. cities in the 1980s, he shot a 13-year-old drug dealer in a North Philadelphia neighborhood as he let a customer inspect his product. The youngster—"Kojak"—told Richards that his father, a heroin addict, had died of AIDS.

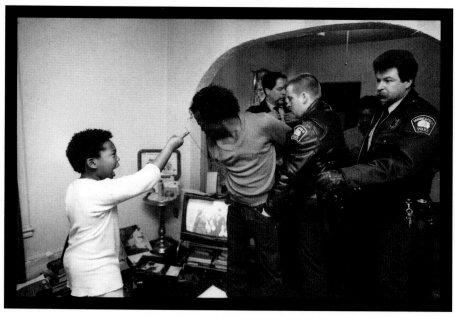

Above:
**CRACK FOR SALE,
5/90**
Eugene Richards

**DOMESTIC VIOLENCE,
10/88**
Donna Ferrato

TO ADVOCATE

CHILDREN OF COPSA MICA, 2/90
Anthony Suau

BLEAK HOUSE

In February 1990, TIME photographer Anthony Suau journeyed to Romania, only two months after the overthrow and death of the nation's longtime communist boss, Nicolae Ceausescu. Suau returned with indelible images of the government's degradation of Romania's land and people, conditions that were tolerated throughout the Soviet bloc. Evidence of Romania's plight, shielded from foreign eyes by the Ceausescu regime, has been documented in even more damning detail since the collapse of the Soviet Union.

This picture was taken in the small town of Copsa Mica. Its chief industry was tire production; 24 hours a day its smokestacks heaved out noxious, coal-based clouds that caked faces and fingers, cars and houses, grass and trees with endless soot. As a result, babies were born with malformed hearts, children suffered from bronchial asthma, and adults struggled with lead poisoning.

Said Suau: "It took several hours for me to realize that I was still standing on the planet earth. It was as if a gigantic bottle of ink had spilled on the town."

TO ADVOCATE

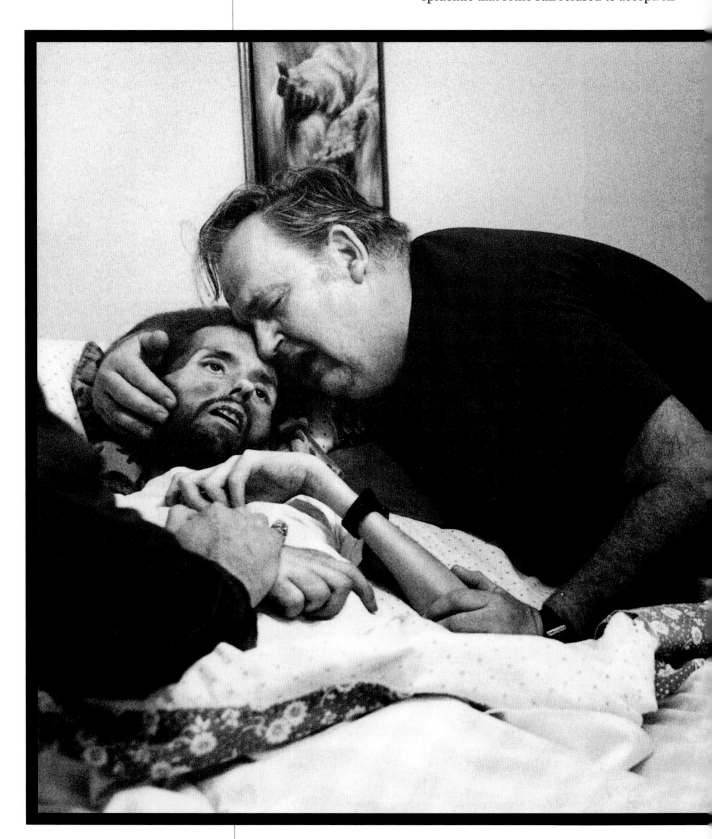

ADVOCACY—OR EXPLOITATION?
When LIFE published Therese Frare's picture of AIDS activist David Kirby on his deathbed, surrounded by his family, the magazine was hailed for putting a human face on a decade-old epidemic that some still refused to accept. As

William Kirby, David's father, told LIFE, "Nobody had ever seen, publicly, how bad it was toward the end." The picture had an unusual second incarnation: designer Tibor Kalman used it in an advertisement for Benetton, the Italian clothing manufacturer. The company claimed its intent was to force the world to turn its eyes to the AIDS crisis—yet although the family had agreed to the picture's use, critics accused Benetton of exploiting suffering for profit.

AIDS PATIENT DAVID KIRBY AND FAMILY, 5/90
Therese Frare

TO ADVOCATE

**A VULTURE STALKS
A STARVING CHILD,
3/93**
Kevin Carter

THE BURDEN OF THE IMAGE

In the 1980s Kevin Carter was one of a crop of young, white South African photographers committed to exposing the brutality of apartheid. But he earned fame in the '90s for his grim picture of a starving girl in Sudan, stalked by an all-too-eager vulture. When it was published in the New York *Times* and TIME,

many readers wrote to ask about the child. Carter had shooed the vulture away, but was not sure if the girl reached her goal, a rescue station.

There was no rescue station for Carter, who came to feel overwhelmed by the images he recorded—even though this picture won the Pulitzer Prize.

When a close friend and fellow photographer was killed in action, Carter's drug abuse heated up. In July, 1994, he was found dead of carbon-monoxide poisoning, a suicide at 33. "I'm really, really sorry," he explained in a note. "The pain of life overrides the joy to the point that joy does not exist."

IT'S A mismatch: on one side, photographer Alon Reininger, armed only with his cameras. On the other side, rifle-toting soldiers of Nicaragua's *Guardia Nacional*, determined to keep his lenses from recording their deeds. Often, great photojournalism comes at a price, in the sheer courage it demands to get a camera close enough to the action to capture it for the world. But like Tom Wolfe's jet pilots who had the "right stuff," the men and women who make it their business to seek out trouble don't like to brag: they let their pictures do the talking.

The patron saint of combat photographers is Robert Capa, whose daring front-line exploits made him a celebrated figure of World War II. He dodged every bullet in five major conflicts—until he was lured back into action by the guerrilla war waged by the Vietnamese against the French in what was then called Indochina. There Capa died, with his boots on, when he stepped on a land mine in 1954.

The cost remains high, but the need to find and share the truth still sends photographers heading straight for the world's danger zones. Their best work is recognized annually by the Overseas Press Club, an organization of U.S. foreign correspondents, with the Robert Capa Gold Medal, for "the best published photographic reporting from abroad requiring exceptional courage and enterprise." Among the photographers who have won this award in recent years are TIME's Anthony Suau, James Nachtwey and Christopher Morris.

Morris has covered 17 conflicts around the world; he was captured by Iranian forces and held prisoner in Baghdad during the Gulf War. But his worst time came far from a combat zone: shooting Russia's "lost generation" in Moscow in 1998, he was hogtied and beaten black-and-blue by thugs after helping his interpreter carry groceries into her apartment.

Nachtwey is a five-time winner of the Capa Medal. In 1994, a week before the historic elections in South Africa, he was one of a group of journalists that was fired on by government troops. As photographer Greg Marinovich fell to the ground, wounded, Nachtwey began pulling him to safety. Then he noticed that another colleague, Ken Oosterbroek, had also been hit. As Nachtwey scrambled to help Oosterbroek, a bullet passed so close to his head that it parted his hair. But Nachtwey's bravery was in vain: Oosterbroek died of his wounds. ■

TO RISK

"If your pictures aren't good enough, you're not close enough. "

– ROBERT CAPA

SOLDIERS CONFRONT PHOTOGRAPHER IN MASAYA, NICARAGUA, 6/79
Matthew Naythons

**IN THE TRENCHES OF
THE WESTERN FRONT,
1917**
Photographer Unknown

 RISK

OUT OF SIGHT, OUT OF MIND

If the Great War—World War I—has faded from our
collective memory by century's end, it is perhaps
because we have very few visual records of this blood-
bath, in which the great European nations sent their
sons off to the trenches to be slaughtered. There's a

reason for the image gap: as Vicki Goldberg notes in her fine study *The Power of Photography* (Abbeville; 1991), "Many—too many—of the photographs that haunt our memories are war photographs, but none come from World War I. Censorship in the Great War was so stringent that for a time civilian photographers were not permitted at the front on pain of death, a rather effective regulation." No wonder this rare shot of British troops racing through the hellish trenches and going "over the top" remains uncredited.

**MOTHER AND CHILD DURING
BOMBING OF MADRID, 1937**
David Seymour

BOMBS BURSTING IN AIR

During a raid by German bombers on Madrid in the Spanish Civil War, photographer David Seymour (known to his colleagues as "Chim") caught a moment of profound irony: a mother nursing her child, even as she eyes the sky for bombs. Seymour was one of the generation of photojournalists who came of age during the historic days of strife in Spain and World War II. After the war, he joined with Robert Capa and others to form a cooperative picture agency, Magnum, that was designed to give photographers more ownership and control of the images they produced. Seymour was killed covering the crisis at the Suez Canal in 1956.

Another founder of Magnum was George Rodger, one of the great combat photographers of World War II. The picture below was taken under fire on Britain's home front in 1943, when Adolf Hitler, unable to invade England by sea, was sending a deadly new weapon—the V-1 missile—to rain death on Londoners.

**LONDON
BLITZ, 1943**
George Rodger

TO RISK

**D-DAY, OMAHA BEACH,
6/6/44**
Robert Capa

Left:

**DEATH OF A LOYALIST
SOLDIER, 1938**
Robert Capa

THE FACE OF WAR

Robert Capa (1913-54) was a self-invented individual, a man who created an idealized vision of what he hoped to become—and then became it. Born Andrei Friedmann in Budapest, he was exiled from Hungary at 18 for his left-leaning politics. He studied in Berlin in the early 1930s, but when the Nazis came to power he left to pursue freelance photography in Paris. There he and his Polish fiancé Gerda Taro invented "Robert Capa"—a supposedly wealthy American photographer—as a sort of brand name to bring higher prices for Friedmann's pictures.

The name may have been bogus; Capa's courage wasn't. In pursuit of pictures that captured combat at closer range than ever before,

Capa headed straight for the front lines, from the Spanish Civil War—where his picture of a soldier just hit by a bullet brought him international fame—to Japan's invasion of China, to the African and European fronts in World War II and on to the birth of the state of Israel in 1948.

Capa went ashore with the first wave of troops on D-day, and his photographs are among the best we have of that momentous event. But a great treasure was lost when a lab assistant ruined Capa's negatives: of his four rolls of D-day shots, only eleven were saved, and they were blurred. When the pictures Capa had risked his life to take appeared, the captions claimed they were out of focus because his hands had been shaking.

ON THE BEACH

The date is Feb. 19, 1945; it is D-day on Iwo Jima, the Japanese-held island only 750 miles from Tokyo. Control of the island, only eight miles square, was vital to the Japanese, and they had packed it with 21,000 men and heavy artillery sheltered in massive bunkers.

American planes bombed the island for 72 days, while destroyers and cruisers lobbed shells into its jungles. But the air attack—and even three days of heavy fire by a special bombardment group from the U.S. Fifth Fleet—left the Japanese unchastened and unsoftened. It was time to send in the Marines.

D-day dawned clear on a calm sea black with 800 U.S. ships. The first landing craft nosed into Futatsune Beach at 9 a.m.; opposition was thin and scattered. As TIME correspondent Robert Sherrod reported, "two hours after the original landings, we had a toe hold and it looked like a good one. But all hell broke loose before noon. From the north and from the south the hidden Japs poured artillery and 6-in. mortars into the Marines on the beachhead ... It was sickening to watch the Jap mortar shells crash into the men as they climbed. These huge explosive charges—'floating ash cans' we called them—would crash among the thin lines of Marines ... By noon the assault battalions reported 20% to 25% fatalities."

Photographer Joe Rosenthal took this shot of the troops charging ashore; weeks later he took the classic shot on page 67 of Marines triumphantly hoisting the Stars and Stripes over the island.

D-DAY ON IWO JIMA, 2/19/45
Joe Rosenthal

SNAKE CHARMER, 1998
Renée Owens

BLUE SHARK, 1993
Nick Caloyianis

IN YOUR FACE!

Sharks and snakes and photos … oh, my! Well, somebody has to take the pictures that make for an eventful journey for us armchair explorers who read *National Geographic*. But the images that result are so hair-raising—like an anaconda's maw, gaping at us from only 12 in. away— that we may forget that some poor devil had to get a camera mighty close to the snake to take it. So in these two pictures, we go backstage and pay attention to the man behind the curtain.

The gentleman embracing the anaconda (or is it the other way around?) is Robert Caputo, a photographer who specializes in natural history. On assignment for the *Geographic* on Venezuela's Orinoco River, he tangled with this 14-footer under the watchful eye of his wife Renée Owens. In addition to taking pictures of the big snakes— which attack animals as large as full-grown deer, squeezing them to death before ingesting them—Caputo and Owens study their reproductive habits, which are little under- stood. The largest anaconda they encountered weighed 215 lbs. Says Caputo: "Sure, I'm scared of snakes."

In documentary filmmaker Nick Caloyianis' picture above, scientist Wes Pratt is photographing a blue shark off the coast of Rhode Island. Blue sharks are voracious and active: adults may reach 15 ft. in length. In a long career, Caloyianis has been attacked only once, by a bull shark in Mexican waters—and he blames that event on an inexperienced crew member who aggravated the animal.

IN HARM'S WAY

In November 1998 James Nachtwey went to Jakarta, Indonesia, on assignment for TIME. Months earlier the government of longtime dictator Suharto had toppled, and religious and ethnic tensions were still high. In two days of rioting, angry Muslim mobs killed 13 Christians. In this picture a Christian man is pursued down a narrow alleyway by a Muslim crowd wielding machetes, metal spikes and bamboo staves.

Nachtwey came upon a chilling scene later: a badly beaten victim of a mob was being held down, with a

STREET RIOTS IN JAKARTA, 11/22/98
James Nachtwey

knife pointed at his throat. The photographer pleaded
with the would-be killer and convinced him to stop,
but the victim died of his wounds. Nachtwey's pictures
from Indonesia were awarded the Robert Capa Gold
Medal by the Overseas Press Club of America.

TO RISK

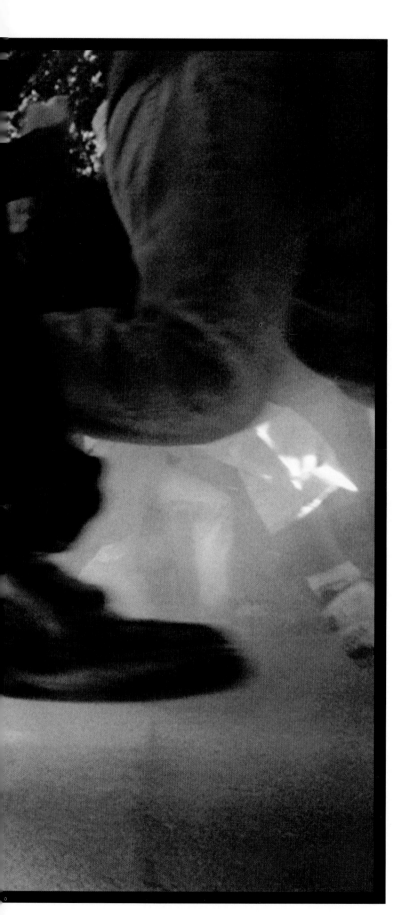

The month must be July, the setting must be Pamplona, Spain, and the young daredevils who are running through the streets just ahead of the charging bulls must be very courageous or very drunk on cheap red wine, or both. And as for photographer Jim Hollander: well, he must be happy he made it out alive.

This scene took place in the seventh running of the bulls during Pamplona's week-long San Fermin festival. In this picture, a fallen runner is crawling for a barrier; behind him a sprinter leading a pack of bulls jumps over another man who has fallen to the ground.

The brave (or is the term foolhardy?) young men who essay this annual ritual may enter it in a spirit of joy. But along the route, one suspects, they might find themselves in a position similar to that of Robert Capa at Omaha Beach. When the German fire was heaviest, he reports in his book *Slightly Out of Focus* (Henry Holt; 1947), "I just stayed behind my tank, repeating a little sentence from my Spanish Civil War days, *Es una cosa muy seria*—'This is a very serious business.'"

TO RISK

TORNADO COMING
5/3/99
J. Pat Carter

T W I S T E R !

In the 1990s a new flock of cameramen—
the storm chasers—is carrying on the
gutsy tradition of the great combat
photographers of World War II. But the
images they record are not the struggles
of man at war, but of man against nature.

On May 3, 1999, enormous supercell
thunderstorms roared through parts of
"Tornado Alley" in Oklahoma, Kansas
and Texas, breeding deadly whirlwinds.
Starting at 5 p.m. and continuing for
20 hours, scores of twisters—brewing
so fast that the exact count is uncertain—
scoured the region. Among them was a
behemoth almost a mile in width, with
wind speeds clocked at 318 m.p.h.—the
fastest wind ever recorded on earth.
The final toll in Oklahoma alone: 41 dead
and 750 injured.

Veteran storm chaser J. Pat Carter led
a mother and her two children to cover
under a freeway overpass near New-
castle, Okla., then snapped the shutter
as two twisters—one a giant—loomed on
the horizon. Carter, the mother and
children were spared.

EXPLORE

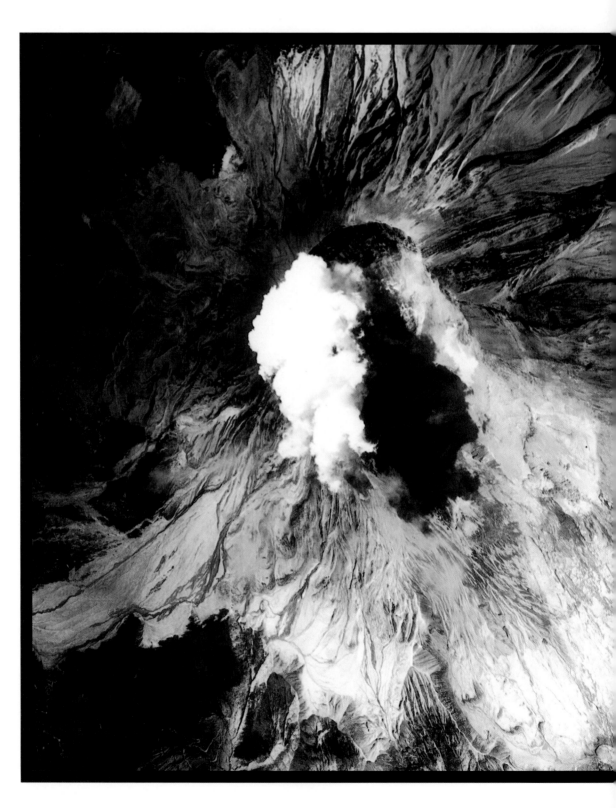

MOUNT ST. HELENS 6/19/80
NASA

WHAT IN THE world *is* that? A satellite picture of a hurricane's eye? A computerized view of an undersea thermal vent? A CAT scan of a blood clot? The possibilities multiply, for in our time photographs have given us countless new ways to see. They are tools of discovery—as in the image at left, an infrared view of Mount St. Helens erupting in 1980, recorded by a camera aboard a U-2 aircraft flying over Washington State at 60,000 ft.

Science uses the camera both to record and to conduct exploration. In the first case, the picture documents one's achievement in managing to place a camera where no camera has ever been before. From inside the womb to orbiting the moon, from Mount Everest's peak to the *Titanic's* grave at the bottom of the sea, the picture stakes a claim: "Been there. Done that."

In the second case, the camera becomes the means of discovery, a tool that reveals aspects of nature we may never have seen before—or could never see, given the limitations of human vision. Photographs have taken us inside the skin (X rays, 1896), inside the atom (the positron was discovered via film in 1932), outside the range of visible light (infrared photography was developed in the 1930s). Pictures stop bullets in flight, magnify ants into monsters, find lost cities in the desert. We use cameras to look for oil, to locate disease, to forecast the weather. Along the way, the means of realizing the information has changed: once we captured light on film; now we capture data with digits. The newish term imaging reflects that evolution.

There's another kind of discovery at work here, for photographs that enlarge our knowledge can also expand our consciousness. The first vision of the whole earth seen from space gave us a new appreciation of the fragile beauty of the planet we share—even as the first vision of the complexity of the human embryo helped us appreciate the mystery and beauty of our coming here. ◾

ICEBOUND

In the century's first decades, the grand (and grandstanding) breed of old-fashioned amateur explorers enjoyed a last hurrah. Robert E. Peary and Dr. Frederick Cook argued over who first reached the North Pole, and their debate still strikes sparks today. The race to the South Pole was settled when Roald Amundsen beat Robert Scott to the prize in 1911.

Photography was an important element of all these journeys—including the ill-fated expedition led by Britain's Ernest Shackleton, which set out in 1914 to achieve one of the last of the "firsts": crossing Antarctica on foot. The group's mobile base camp was the three-masted *Endurance*, specially made to crash through the polar ice. And that she did, until the ship was trapped amid fast-freezing ice. Shackleton set off for help. After a series of ordeals, including navigating a lifeboat 800 miles through heavy seas, he managed to rescue his 27 stranded crewmen—and the pictures of Frank Hurley, cached in the ice for safekeeping. Undaunted, Hurley continued to take his camera to remote locations, including Papua New Guinea, before his death in 1962.

ICEBOUND *ENDURANCE,* **1915**
Frank Hurley

Right:
***ENDURANCE* CRUSHED BY THE ICE, 1915**
Frank Hurley

STILL LIFE WITH BULLET

Maybe man can't stop time. But in the work of scientist-photographer Harold Edgerton, time is man-handled, caught in the act, exposed as a series of discrete events, and an entire new world of eerie, slow-motion beauty is revealed. Edgerton invented the strobe light to study high-speed phenomena; the power of his images was a happy bonus. Here, the passage of a bullet through an apple becomes a study in color and shape. (Yes, Edgerton had an artist's eye—the apple is posed on a cartridge.) In this picture the 30-cal. projectile is moving at 2,900 ft. per sec.; the flash exposure (faster than a speeding bullet!) lasted one-third of one-millionth of a second. A microphone, triggered by the gun's report, set off the stroboscopic flash.

**GARDEN ANT WITH
APHID, 1996**
Andrew Syred

Left:
**WHAT WOULD
WILLIAM TELL
THINK? 1964**
Dr. Harold E. Edgerton

READY FOR HIS CLOSE-UP

Just as Edgerton's strobe flash revealed a new world of slow motion, the advent of electron-microscope photography enlarged our sense of nature's complexity: insects became monsters out of science fiction, and deadly viruses appeared as brilliant skeins of colored cells. The scanning electron microscope, developed in the 1930s, is the anti-Hubble: the wonders it reveals, while every bit as unexpected and awe-inspiring, reveal a world within our world, not far beyond it.

These pictures, like Edgerton's, do double duty: we amateurs enjoy them for their utter strangeness, while scientists employ them to advance the study of medicine, genetics, physics, chemistry, biology, zoology … the list goes on. This picture of a garden ant carrying a rose aphid in its mouth parts captures a symbiotic partnership. Ants herd the aphids on domestic rose plants and collect honeydew from them; in return, ants protect aphids by removing their predators' eggs.

ASCENDING EVEREST, 5/96
Neal Beidleman

THE PROOF IS ON THE FILM

In perhaps the century's most memorable achievement in old-fashioned exploring, New Zealander Edmund Hillary and Sherpa Tenzing Norkay, above, climbed to the summit of Mount Everest on May 29, 1953. They took a camera to provide indisputable proof of their accomplishment—as had an earlier British explorer, George Mallory, who famously declared he wanted to climb Everest "because it is there." Mallory and climbing companion Andrew Irvine were lost on the mountain in 1924, and no one knows if they reached the top before they died.

For decades other Everest climbers searched for the bodies of Mallory and Irvine. Finally, a 1999 expedition led by veteran American climber Eric Simonson retraced Mallory's old route on Everest's Tibetan, or north, face—and found his body on a rocky, windswept slope, some 2,000 ft. below the summit. But Simonson's group failed to find the one thing that might solve the question of whether or not Mallory and Irvine had reached Everest's top: Mallory's folding Kodak camera. If the pair made it to the summit, they would undoubtedly have photographed themselves there—and those images might well be retrievable from film kept in so deep a freeze.

The photo at left was taken by Neal Beidleman, a guide on one of the ill-fated expeditions that sought Everest's summit in May 1996. Eight climbers died in a period of 24 hours when a howling blizzard engulfed the mountain's peak.

TO EXPLORE

WOMB WITH A VIEW

As certainly as NASA's first photographs of the whole earth changed the way we view our planet, Swedish photographer Lennart Nilsson's first photographs of a living human embryo changed the way we view life before birth—and provided a new visual element in America's heated debate over the ethics of abortion. First published in LIFE in 1965—after Nilsson had worked seven years to accomplish them—the photos opened our eyes to both the complexity and magisterial beauty of the human fetus.

In the picture at right, an 18-week-old fetus sucks its thumb, training for the suckling action it will employ after birth. At this age, the fetus is about 8 in. long from crown to rump; it is active and energetic, and its mother can generally feel it kicking. Its fingernails are dangerously long and can scratch the thin skin of the face.

In the picture below, Nilsson caught the moment a sperm cell (blue) penetrates the egg cell (yellow). Of some 200 million sperm cells that race toward the ovum, only one will penetrate and fertilize the egg, which is 90,000 times as large as the sperm.

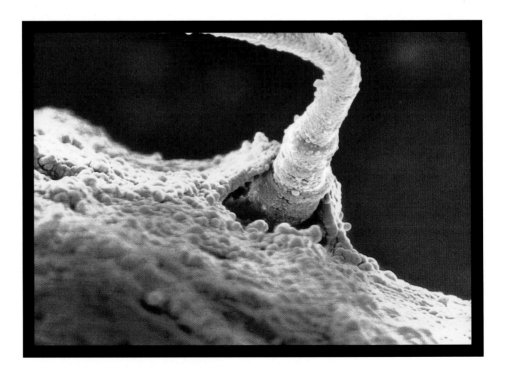

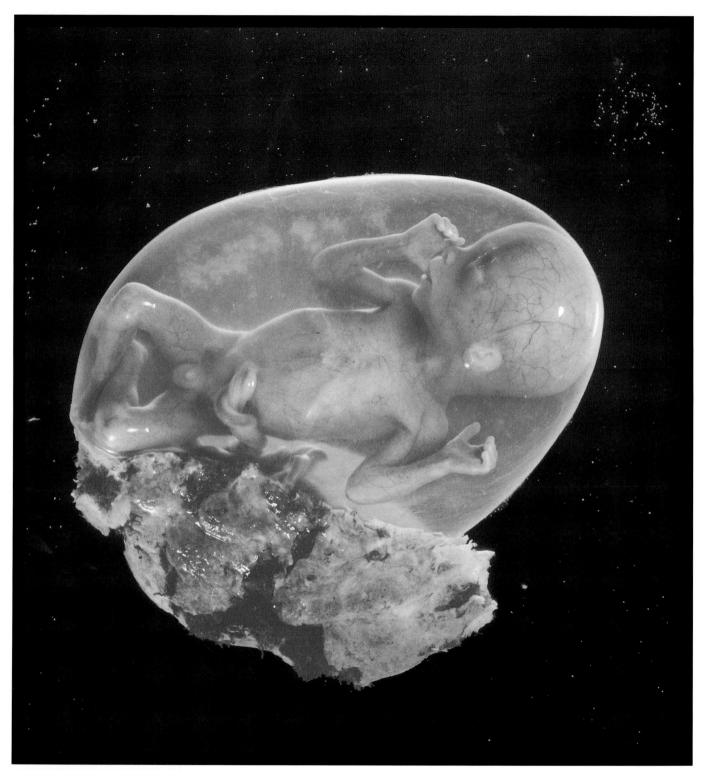

HUMAN EMBRYO, 18 WEEKS, 1964
Lennart Nilsson

Left:
SPERM MEETS EGG, 1988
Lennart Nilsson

EARTHRISE FROM THE
MOON, 12/24/68
William Anders

Right:
JOHN GLENN BLASTS
OFF IN THE SPACE
SHUTTLE, 10/29/98
Mark M. Lawrence

A FRESH PERSPECTIVE

For Americans, 1968 unspooled as a calendar of horrors. January brought
the Tet offensive, deepening the U.S. quagmire in Vietnam. Spring
arrived—and Martin Luther King and Robert Kennedy were murdered.
In August police clashed with protesting kids in Chicago. But Christmas
Eve brought a reprieve, as eyes gazed in wonder on pictures that put
the world's woes into perspective: three U.S. astronauts aboard the
Apollo 8 spacecraft showed the earth rising over the surface of the moon
as they read passages from *Genesis* to an enthralled, grateful nation.

PIONEER'S RETURN

The final frontier? Science-fiction fans assure us it is space, but in a century that has witnessed vast steps forward in our understanding of life before birth and of disease and its causes, one of the least explored regions of human terrain is the aging process. So when former Senator John Glenn, the first U.S. astronaut to orbit the earth, lifted off in the shuttle *Discovery* in October 1998, at age 77, it was a pioneering moment in the study of mankind as well as space. As Glenn put it, he was flying not for glory but for geriatric science. During the mission, his blood was drawn, his sleep cycles measured, his balance and heart function gauged. As NASA boss Daniel Goldin said, in classic tech-talk, "John Glenn represents a sample beyond our experience domain."

TO EXPLORE

Massively hyped, gravely flawed and then triumphantly redeemed, the Hubble Space Telescope is the tragic hero of America's space program. Ballyhooed as the cutting edge of a brilliant new age of astronomy, it suffered a series of mishaps. First its launch was slowed by NASA's tragic *Challenger* explosion. Then, shortly after the "big eye" went into orbit 370 miles above the earth and its distorting atmosphere in 1990, NASA revealed that the telescope's optical mirror had been incorrectly ground, and its images were out of focus. Soon other problems—from faulty gyroscopes to shuddering solar panels—struck the Hubble.

So NASA sent in the cavalry. In 1993 seven astronauts blasted off on a complex mission: to sharpen the scope's marred eyesight and fix its support systems. They succeeded, and since then professional and amateur astronomers alike have marveled at the glorious images that have resolved on the Hubble's mirror. The picture at right shows the object M2-9, a "butterfly," or bipolar planetary, nebula in the constellation Ophiucus, also known as the "Siamese Squid" or "Twinjet Nebula."

In 1991 the Magellan spacecraft orbiting the planet Venus sent back to Earth a radar image of the planet's second tallest peak, the five-mile-high volcano Maat Mons, below. Its lava flow shows up as as lighter yellow in this computer-realized image; the colors are based on hues recorded by Soviet Venera spacecraft.

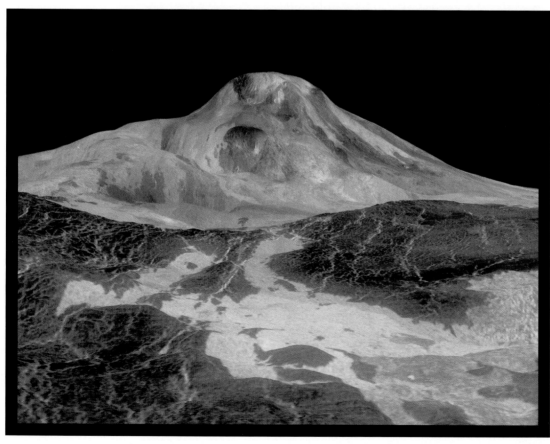

MAAT MONS, VENUS, 1991
Jet Propulsion Laboratory

Right:

"TWINJET NEBULA" FROM HUBBLE TELESCOPE, 8/2/97
Space Telescope Science Institute

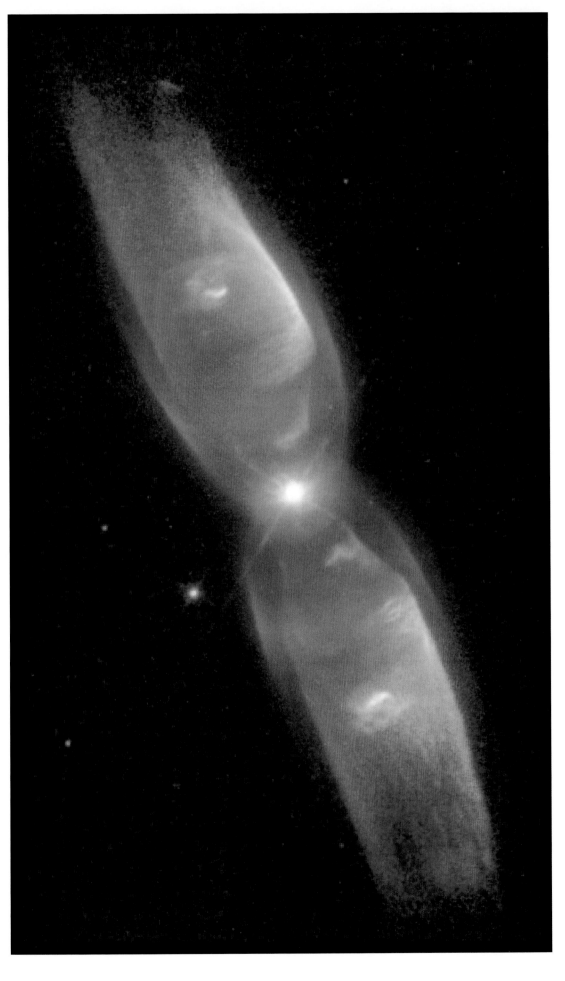

TO EXPLORE

JOURNEY'S END

One of the century's most memorable disasters, the sinking of the *Titanic* on its maiden voyage in 1912, was not captured on film. But 73 years later, an expedition led by explorer Robert D. Ballard traveled to the bottom of the North Atlantic and returned with some of the most unexpected images of our time: photographs of the great luxury liner at rest on the bottom of the sea. After decades of romanticizing, speechifying and moralizing had freighted the ship with a mighty cargo of metaphor (and this was *before* the blockbuster movie), it was as if Ballard had managed to catch Moby Dick sporting for his camera.

Ballard's journey to the bottom of the sea was partially funded by the U.S. Navy, which has a strong interest in deep-sea technology. He found *Titanic* 10 miles east of the location radioed from the sinking ship after its iceberg encounter.

Titanic rests 13,000 ft. underwater; to find her, Ballard employed a remote unmanned submersible, the *Argo*, which was tethered to a ship on the surface. (An observer likened finding the *Titanic* with the *Argo* to "dangling a needle into a soda bottle from the top of the Empire State Building.") The size of a small car, the *Argo* carried three cameras in front and a battery of strobe lights behind, for illumination. In the first four days after the ship and a "debris field" stretching a mile behind the wreck were found, the *Argo* and a smaller vehicle (note the lights in the picture) shot some 20,000 frames of film. At last, *Titanic* enjoyed a photo-op.

THE WRECK OF THE *TITANIC*, 9/85
Emory Kristof

TO EXPLORE

When first introduced, high-level aerial photography provided valuable data to both soldiers and scientists. The Cuban missile crisis of 1962 began when U.S. U-2 planes, flying high over the island, shot pictures that clearly showed Soviet missiles being deployed in the jungle. Satellite images are now used in weather forecasting, environmental science and geological exploration. But few would have predicted that aerial photography would prove a powerful tool for archae-ologists, as it did in the discovery of Ubar.

The ancient, fabled center of Africa's frankincense trade, Ubar had long been lost, covered by the desert sands—until scientists used microwave satellite images to find caravan tracks that lie just below the surface of the desert and are invisible from the ground. The tracks converge on a spot in Oman's "Empty Quarter," where scientists dug into the ground in 1992—and found the ruins of the city. In the computer-colorized picture below, the magenta-colored areas at the top are large sand dunes. The green areas are limestone rocks that form the desert floor. The trade routes appear as thin red streaks.

TO **EXPLORE**

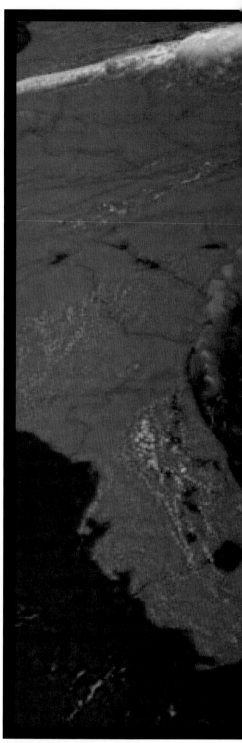

HURRICANE BONNIE, 9/98
NASA/Goddard Lab for Atmospheres

Left:
THE LOST CITY OF UBAR, 8/3/95
Jet Propulsion Laboratory/Caltech

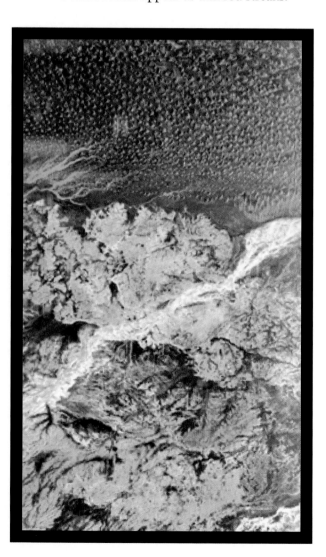

THE SPIRAL MENACE

The advent of satellite photography has given us a new sense of the enormous scale of earth's weather patterns. Here, as Hurricane Bonnie hovers off America's East Coast in September 1998, its swirling winds form a spiral that extends from Florida to Maine. But even with such high-flying new tools, forecasters struggle to predict a storm's progress. As Bonnie hovered offshore, hundreds of thousands of coast dwellers moved into full alert—but the storm fizzled out. Weeks later, Hurricane Mitch roared through Central America, leaving a trail of destruction and killing more than 11,000 people.

REVEAL

**""I have to be
as much a
diplomat as a
photographer.""**

**— ALFRED

EISENSTAEDT**

THE CAMERA loved Marilyn Monroe—and Marilyn loved posing, according to veteran celebrity photographer Eve Arnold, in whose studio the picture at right was taken. In Hollywood, where control of the star's image is all important, a studio session can be a show in itself, requiring technicians, assistants, makeup artists, caterers—not to mention the star's entourage (Monroe brought a gang of seven friends to lend support at this shoot). Recalling that day in her book *Marilyn Monroe: An Appreciation* (Knopf; 1987), Arnold tells us that it took three or four hours simply to prepare the star for the camera: because she was to pose in a bikini and a slip, full-body makeup was required, including shading and highlights. "When Marilyn finally emerged from the dressing room, she was sparkling: hair, face, body, fingernails and toenails all newly attended to. Her entourage applauded."

Hollywood photographers strive for the same result as veteran TIME cover photographers Gregory Heisler and William Coupon, or legendary portraitists Yousuf Karsh and Arnold Newman: they hope to create an icon, an idealized, almost platonic realization of the subject's essence. But the studio environment is inherently limiting. As Arnold notes, "A studio session … provides the greatest chance for control. [But] even though there is total freedom, I still dislike studio photography and the contrived images that usually stem from this genre." Philippe Halsman, another highly regarded portrait photographer, also chafed at the studio's formality. He finally came up with the notion of asking his subjects to jump at the end of his sessions, hoping the physical movement would help break down the decorum demanded by the situation.

Great portraits have their place: our mental image of Winston Churchill is likely to be Karsh's famous shot of the great man's glowering, bulldog countenance. Yet we crave informality. We demand the uncontrived. We want to see the powerful and the famous with their guard down. More than idealization, we want revelation. And that demands access—not the illicit access of the paparazzi, whose stolen images leave us feeling complicit in the theft of privacy they require. We want the access achieved by photographers who earn the trust of their subjects and return with images that expose their hidden places: X rays of the soul. ∎

MARILYN MONROE, 1960
Eve Arnold

LIFE OF THE PARTY

In the grisly equations used by historians to establish the most prolific mass murderers of the century, Mao Zedong and Joseph Stalin vie for first place. Both initiated policies that forced the starvation of millions of their own people, yet both seemed unfazed by a sense of responsibility. China scholar Jonathan D. Spence caught Mao's complexity in his profile for the TIME 100 series, citing the "curious mixture of jocularity and cruelty, of utopian visions and blinkered perceptions, that lay at the heart of his character."

The picture above was taken in 1963, five years after Mao's Great Leap Forward resulted in a famine that killed more than 20 million Chinese—and three years before his bizarre Cultural Revolution brought suffering or death to millions more. While China wept, the erstwhile guerrilla whiled away his days in the Forbidden City with swimming, young women—and Ping-Pong.

Adolf Hitler's crimes have led us to demonize him. Oversimplifying, we see only a fanatic obsessed by racial theories, a propagandist playing upon his people's worst impulses, the architect of the Final Solution, a man incapable of laughter or joy. Indeed, his public posture was generally rigid, forbidding. But in one moment of supreme triumph he let the mask slip.

TIME's original story set the scene: "It was Friday, June 21, 1940. At exactly 3:15 o'clock, German summer time, from a touring car that had stopped at the far end of the avenue stepped a small man with a catlike tread and a supreme sense of the drama that is history. This was Adolf Hitler's first visit to the Forest of Compiègne, where ... 22 years ago a delegation of Germans signed an armistice dictated by France's Marshal Ferdinand Foch." History had come full circle: Hitler's panzers had cut through France like butter, and he now staged the French surrender on the exact spot of Germany's humiliating surrender in World War I. Near the railroad car where the French were agreeing to his terms, the Führer danced a jig.

TO REVEAL

ADOLF HITLER, 6/21/40
Photographer Unknown

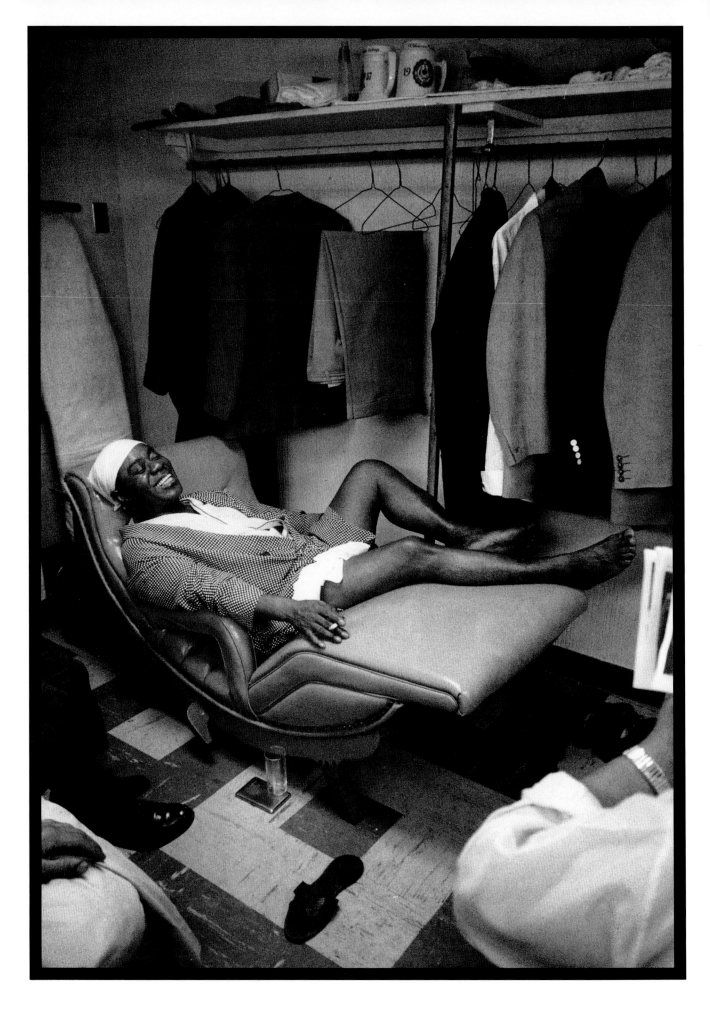

PRIVILEGED GLIMPSES

In 1959 photographer Dennis Stock caught legendary jazzman Louis Armstrong relaxing backstage at Philadelphia's Latin Casino. The exuberant performer—named in 1999 as one of TIME's 100 most influential people of the century—knew how to wind down following an engagement. As a TIME reporter traveling on tour with the trumpeter reported in a 1949 cover story, "After the show, which is usually over between 2 and 4 a.m., he goes out for a 'snack,' accompanied by Brown Sugar, his valet, and whatever old friends and acquaintances want to join the party. The snack usually comes to a huge portion of ham and eggs, with potatoes, hot biscuits, hominy grits and coffee on the side. When complimented on his appetite, Satchmo replies, 'Man, that's just a synopsis.'"

The picture above is surprising for two reasons: it captures a sly, playful side of artist Georgia O'Keeffe—so often stern in photos—and it is a rare portrait by landscape specialist Ansel Adams.

GEORGIA O'KEEFFE AND ORVILLE COX, 1937
Ansel Adams

Left:
LOUIS ARMSTRONG, 1959
Dennis Stock

LEAPING TO CONCLUSIONS

How to strip away the carefully controlled mask that most of us—and especially those often photographed—present to the camera? One noted portrait photographer came up with a unique solution: at the conclusion of his regular sessions, he asked his subjects to take a big jump for his camera. The results—191 celebrated folk caught in the act of defying gravity—were collected in *Philippe Halsmann's Jump Book* (Simon and Schuster, 1959).

In his charming, facetious introduction to the book, Halsman claims "jumpology" is a new branch of psychology, asserting we can learn deep truths about people according to their mid-leap body language. Analyzing Richard Nixon's tightly controlled hop, Halsman points out that Nixon's hands, stretched out for balance, indicate insecurity, "a feeling that life is similar to tightrope walking." Meanwhile, Audrey Hepburn's barefoot, all-embracing exuberance reveals that—well, that it's Audrey jumping.

Far Right:
AUDREY HEPBURN, 1955
Philippe Halsman

RICHARD NIXON, 1955
Philippe Halsman

JAMES DEAN, 3/55
Phil Stern

Right:
ANDY WARHOL, 1986
Phil Stern

These pages record a collision of photography and fame that began with a near collision. Veteran cameraman Phil Stern tells the story of the 1955 picture at left in his book *Phil Stern's Hollywood* (Knopf; 1993): "At 7:30 a.m., I was cruising west on Sunset Boulevard … Coming down Laurel Canyon was a crazy motorcyclist who was driving through a red light. We were on a collision course. We both braked and careered through the intersection. I came close to killing him—just a few inches saved his life. I stuck my head out the window, screaming profanities, as he got up off the bike with a dopey grin on his face. It was James Dean. We ended up having a two-hour breakfast at Schwab's Drug Store, and I invited him over to the *Guys and Dolls* set, where I had a still gallery rigged to shoot Brando and Sinatra. Dean was fascinated by cameras, and came along."

Years later, Stern showed his prints of Dean to another artist who was fascinated by cameras, Andy Warhol—the prophet of today's celebrity-fixated, image-saturated culture. (Note Stern's famous picture of Dean peeking out of the neck of his turtleneck sweater.) Recalling his meeting with Warhol for this book, Stern says, "As Warhol got more and more excited by my pictures, I did something that's a no-no—I took out my Nikon and started shooting hand-held time exposures. Warhol didn't like it one bit, and complained. I said, 'I can't help it, Andy. God constructed me this way, to take pictures.' I was really flattered that he collected my prints—until I found out later he collected *everything*."

A WHALE OF A TALENT

In 1979 a TIME cover story hailed the formidable gifts of a new superstar, opera's Luciano Pavarotti: "No other tenor in modern times has hit the opera world with such seismic force. At 6 ft. and nearly 300 lbs., 'Big P.,' as Soprano Joan Sutherland calls him, is more than life-size, as is everything about him—his clarion high Cs, his fees of $8,000 per night for an opera and $20,000 for a recital, his Rabelaisian zest for food and fun. 'He is not *primo tenore,*' says San Francisco Opera General Director Kurt Herbert Adler. 'He is *primissimo tenore.*' Pavarotti is one of those magnetic performers, like Nureyev in dance and Olivier in theater, who not only please the *cognoscenti* but also wow the masses."

Photographer Enrico Ferorelli shot Pavarotti on vacation at his summer home in Pesaro, Italy, for TIME—and caught the "surprisingly graceful Gargantua" cavorting in his pool. Hearing the tenor vocalize around the house turned out to be a conversion experience for Ferorelli, who recalls, "When I was a child, my parents took me to the opera, but I just didn't enjoy it. When I first heard Pavarotti sing, I rediscovered the beauty of the human voice."

**LUCIANO PAVAROTTI,
8/79**
Enrico Ferorelli

The roar of the crowd! The joy of victory! The glitz of superstardom! Michael Jordan knew them all—and here we see him enjoying the glamorous life of a pro athlete on the road, as captured by veteran sports photographer Walter Iooss Jr. in the book *Rare Air* (HarperCollins; 1993). The lonely Bull is bathing a pesky sprained ankle in a vast, impersonal hotel suite in Orlando. As Iooss recalled the scene, "I was amazed by his dedication … Every 90 seconds he would switch from hot to cold water. Then he took ultrasound treatments. He did this all through the next day. Finally he put on shoes to see if he could walk. That night he scored 36 points."

**MICHAEL JORDAN,
2/93**
Walter Iooss Jr.

"They are leaders who have made a difference.
Not because they wished it, but because they willed it."

-RN

**FOUR PRESIDENTS AT THE DEDICATION OF THE
RICHARD NIXON LIBRARY AND BIRTHPLACE 7/90**
Diana Walker

DOUBLE TAKE

You're right—four of the figures here aren't statues. And the setting isn't Madame Tussaud's wax museum—it's the Richard Nixon Library and Birthplace in Yorba Linda, Calif., where three former Presidents and one sitting President, George Bush, gathered in 1990 for the building's dedication. Among the items on view that day was a display of 30 of the 56 TIME covers on which Nixon had then appeared; he is the person most often featured on the magazine's cover.

TIME White House photographer Diana Walker—a well-known face to these veterans of the Oval Office—caught this picture as they surveyed a room displaying bronze-tone life-size statues of 10 world leaders: from left, Zhou Enlai and Mao Zedong (seated), Leonid Brezhnev, Nikita Khrushchev, Anwar Sadat, Golda Meir (obscured behind Bush), Winston Churchill, Charles de Gaulle, Konrad Adenauer and Yoshida Shigeru. Is it our imagination, or does each man play his role to perfection—good soldiers Gerald Ford and Ronald Reagan hitting their marks perfectly; Nixon scheming away with a telltale hand-washing gesture; the preppy Bush trying to figure out a stance that's casual, yet prudent.

TIME's Lance Morrow caught the aspiration behind the scene in the final paragraph of his accompanying story: "Trying to hurry history's verdict, Nixon has always had a habit of dressing the set with giants, setting the delay timer and then jumping into the picture himself."

RONALD REAGAN
AND MIKHAIL
GORBACHEV,
10/12/86
David Hume Kennerly

Below:
BILL CLINTON AND
MONICA LEWINSKY,
10/96
Dirck Halstead

STAR WARS SINKS THE SUMMIT

In the autumn of 1986 Ronald Reagan and Mikhail Gorbachev met for a summit conference in Reykjavík, Iceland. The stakes were high: Reagan, who had angered Gorbachev by calling the Soviet Union "an evil empire," was hoping to emerge with the most sweeping arms-control agreement in the history of the nuclear age. But in its last half an hour, the agreement was scuttled by Gorbachev's opposition to Reagan's cherished Star Wars missile defense system. David Hume Kennerly took the picture above moments later, catching the generally upbeat Reagan allowing his anger to show.

TIME got the picture on its cover, scoring an old-fashioned scoop over arch-rival *Newsweek*. The final session of talks was held Sunday, when both news-magazines are printed, and both held their pressruns to cover the story. But TIME had arranged to have a bulky, state-of-the-art photo scanner delivered to Iceland. When the talks broke down, TIME's picture technology team was able to scan the photo and send it via satellite to New York City. The cover ran with the headline NO DEAL: STAR WARS SINKS THE SUMMIT. *Newsweek*, with no scanner on the scene, ran a picture taken earlier, showing both leaders smiling, with a positive headline. Today this kind of race is obsolete: 13 years after the Iceland summit, it took only a few minutes for TIME photographer Christopher Morris to send the picture of Kosovar refugees on page 23 from Albania to New York City—as a digital file attached to an e-mail message.

TO REVEAL

Purgatory for photographers? It just might be shooting White House fund raisers, stagey events almost guaranteed to yield no news. But you never know: witness the picture below, which ran on the cover of TIME in August 1998. How did photographer Dirck Halstead, who has been shooting politicians for TIME for decades, come up with it? Halstead tells the story best, in his online photojournalism magazine (*http//digitaljournalist.org*): "I have a theory that every time the shutter captures a frame, that image is recorded at a very low threshold in the brain of the photographer … as 'photographic lint.' When the photographs of Monica Lewinsky, in her beret on the lawn of the White House emerged, I *knew* I had seen that face with the President. I had no idea when, or where … I hired a researcher, and she started to go through the piles of slides in the light room. After four days, and more than 5,000 slides, she found *one* image, from a fund-raising event in 1996." Gotcha!

IT'S SURPRISING

but true: the world of athletics has given us many memorable images, yet few of the pictures we return to again and again portray actual historic moments in sport. Perhaps that's because the meaning we get out of a sports photo often relies on the knowledge we put into it. Let's face it: a photograph of Michael Jordan's championship-winning basket in the 1998 NBA playoffs against the Utah Jazz really doesn't look much different from any other shot of Michael Jordan scoring a basket. It's the information in the caption ("Champs again!"), not the information in the picture, that makes it historic. That's why an image that shows no action at all, like the famous shot in this chapter of Babe Ruth, can be a classic of sports photography. It's just a picture of a man from behind, but we know that this is the Babe's last appearance at Yankee Stadium, and that he is soon to die.

The other images of sport that endure through the years are those that capture the essence of a particular athlete's style: Joe DiMaggio's beautifully balanced swing, or Jim Brown busting through a clutch of tacklers on a muddy field, fighting the elements as much as his opponents. We're also drawn to pictures that manage to isolate the passions that bring us to sport in the first place: effort, endurance, grace, pride in the body and joy in the contest. The famous shot of Roger Bannister's finish of the first sub-four-minute mile is the rare photo that works on two levels, combining the news of a historic event with a moving portrait of exhaustion and triumph.

Most of all, we enjoy photographs that find the sense of play that's beneath the surface of all athletics—like the picture here of kids in a stickball game on a summer day in Brooklyn in the '50s. It was taken by Garry Winogrand, whose later work is celebrated for its alienated take on the American scene. But in his rookie days in photography, Winogrand prowled the streets of New York, shooting for SPORTS ILLUSTRATED and other magazines, and here his camera is completely in synch with the scene it records. Interesting that—for all the strenuous hoopla surrounding the major leagues—this picture captures the essence of the sport in a stripped-down, mongrel version of the game, where the field is concrete, home plate is a manhole cover and the ball is a rubber "pinkie." ∎

STICKBALL IN BROOKLYN, 8/59
Garry Winogrand

TO CHEER

JESSE OWENS, BERLIN OLYMPICS, 8/8/36
Anthony Camerano

The Olympics are intended to be a celebration of international unity, but all too often the Games are as memorable for the posturing on the podium as the action in the arena. That's the case with these two pictures, which reflect one of the central themes of the century, the politics of race.

Adolf Hitler envisioned the Berlin Games of 1936 as a showcase for Nazi Germany and Caucasian athletic superiority. But Hitler's grand Aryan pageant was derailed by a black American, Jesse Owens, who became the first athlete to win four gold medals at the Games. At left, Owens salutes the American flag after winning the broad jump, while runner-up Carl Ludwig Long of Germany offers a Nazi salute. Rounding out this highly politicized portrait of the "family of man" is bronze medalist Naoto Tajima of Japan.

Thirty-two years later, the tables were turned: U.S. blacks Tommie Smith, center, and John Carlos ignore the U.S. flag and give a black-power salute after winning gold and silver medals in the 200-m run at the 1968 Mexico City Games. When they were suspended from the team, other blacks threatened a walk-out, but Jesse Owens stepped in to prevent it.

**BLACK POWER,
MEXICO CITY
OLYMPICS,
10/16/68**
Neil Leifer

WHEN ART MEETS PROPAGANDA

The beautiful study of athletes in motion above was taken by one of the most controversial 20th century photographers, Leni Riefenstahl. As TIME described her in a 1936 cover story, "By 1930 she was one of [Germany's] leading cinema stars, noted for her daring in playing dangerous sequences without a double ... In 1934 she met Adolf Hitler, who had long admired her work. He commissioned her to make the official film of last summer's Nürnberg Party Congress in which she directed 800,000 men." That film, *Triumph of the*

Will, is a masterwork, a disturbing marriage of art and propaganda. It was followed by the beautiful *Olympia,* her film of the 1936 Berlin Olympics, for which the photograph above was taken.

A figure from a vanished past? Not quite. In March 1998, a murmur ran through the crowd at TIME's 75th-anniversary party, where Bill and Hillary Clinton, Muhammad Ali, Bill Gates, John Glenn, Joe Di Maggio, Steven Spielberg and Toni Morrison were among the guests: Leni Riefenstahl, age 95, had just walked into the room.

ARMS AND THE MAN

The picture below has a wonderful documentary quality: it shows crewmen of the U.S.S. *Monterey* enjoying a basketball game in the big carrier's forward elevator during World War II. Yes, the photograph is a fine study in sunlight and shadow. Yes, it offers a strong interplay of forms. Yes, it reminds us that a workout is a godsend to the stressed-out. But what's most fun about this picture is that it has a secret: the player at left jumping for the ball is Ensign Gerald R. Ford, future President of the United States.

NIGHT START OF THE DECATHLON, 8/36
Leni Riefenstahl

Right:
PLAYING BASKETBALL ON AN AIRCRAFT CARRIER, 6/44
Victor Jorgensen

DAMN (GOOD) YANKEES

Love 'em, hate 'em or damn 'em—if you're a baseball fan, you have an opinion about the New York Yankees. But even die-hard Yankee haters concede that many of the game's greatest memories come in pinstripes. Among them is Nat Fein's Pulitzer prizewinning picture of "Babe Ruth Day" in 1948 at Yankee Stadium, only two months before the beloved slugger's death. Though it's one of the most moving pictures of baseball, it shows no action, or even its subject's face. But it captures the sweet sadness of sport, a sadness that has everything to do with vanished youth—of the "boys of summer"—and of their fans.

When Joe DiMaggio died at 84 in 1999, sportswriters searched for the reason he kept a grip on our imagination for decades after he retired in 1951, following a war-abbreviated career of only 13 years. Baseball maven Daniel Okrent ran quickly through the checklist in TIME: "Yes, he was noble, and he looked great and he married Marilyn Monroe." But one thread appeared in almost every story, including Okrent's: DiMaggio's grace as a player, both in the outfield and at the plate. That perfection of form is captured in the picture at right of the finish of his swing. His arms are extended, his stride is long, his eyes are fixed on the ball as it soars away from his bat, no doubt bound for deep left-center field, where only one man in the game could catch up to it—the one watching its flight.

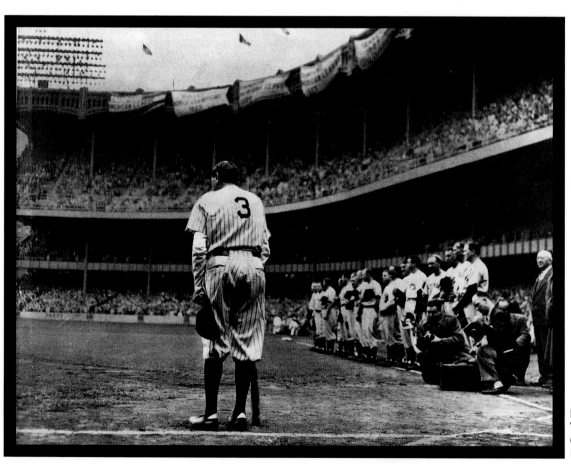

BABE RUTH DAY AT YANKEE STADIUM, 6/13/48
Nat Fein

JOE DI MAGGIO,
4/29/41
Photographer Unknown

TO CHEER

ROGER BANNISTER BREAKS THE FOUR-MINUTE MILE, 5/6/54
L. Blanford

BEAT THE CLOCK

We love running for its simplicity: the only gear it requires comes factory-installed. And we love this picture because it shows one of the historic, well, milestones in track: the breaking of the four-minute mile. Athletes began to focus on this Everest for the fleet-of-foot when Paavo Nurmi clocked in at 4:10.4 in 1923. Sweden's Gunder ("the Wonder") Hägg ran a breathtaking 4:01.4 in 1945. But there the clock stopped. Meanwhile, Roger Bannister, who began running in the early '50s as a third-string miler at Britain's Oxford University, had set his sights on the prize. Improving rapidly, he finished fourth at the 1952 summer Olympics; at the end of 1953, he ran 4:03.6 mile.

In May 1954, at Oxford's rural Iffley Road Track, Bannister went for the record. In TIME's original account, "Some 300 yds. from the finish, [he] began pouring it on, lengthening his stride for his famed finishing kick, his head rolled back, his neck painfully arched. He tore the tape and collapsed unconscious … Over the loudspeakers came the meticulous voice of the announcer: 'A time which is a new meeting and track record, and which, subject to ratification, will be a new English native, a British national, a British all comers, European, British Empire and world record. The time was three …' At that point the 1,500 track fans in the stands broke into such an uproar that the rest of the announcement was lost: 'Three minutes, fifty-nine and four-tenths seconds.'"

**CASSIUS CLAY BEATS SONNY LISTON,
5/25/65**
Neil Leifer

PICTURE SOURCES

COVER/TABLE OF CONTENTS/INTRODUCTION
Front Cover: (Earthrise) NASA, (Iwo Jima) AP/Wide
World Photos, (Muhammad Ali) Neil Leifer,
(Shuttle blast-off) Mark M. Lawrence **Back Cover:**
Christopher Morris/Black Star for TIME **iv** Magnum
Photos, Steve Liss, New York *Daily News*, Contact
Press Images, **v** W. Eugene Smith courtesy Black
Star, Reuters/Archive Photos, Albert Bonniers Forlag
AB, *A Child Is Born*, Dell Publishing Company, CPi,
Allsport **vi** AP/Wide World Photos, AP/Wide World
Photos **1** AP/Wide World Photos, LIFE Magazine
©Time Inc. **2** ©Harold and Esther Edgerton
Foundation, 1999, courtesy of Palm Press, Sygma,
3 Magnum Photos, Library of Congress

TO WITNESS
4-5 AP/Wide World Photos **6-7** AP/Wide World
Photos **8** Magnum Photos **10** AP/Wide World
Photos **11** *Bild Zeitung* **12** LIFE Magazine ©Time
Inc. **13** AP/Wide World Photos **14-15** Corbis-
Bettmann **16** Magnum Photos **16-17** Gamma
Liaison **18-19** Magnum Photos **20-21** Halifax *Daily
News*/Sipa Press **21** Sygma **22-23** Black Star

TO DOCUMENT
24-25 Edward Curtis, *An Oasis in the Bad Lands*,
1905/Philadelphia Museum of Art; purchased with
funds from the American Museum of Photography
26-27 Library of Congress **28-29** National Museum
of Finland/Finnish Evangelical Lutheran Mission
30 Culver Pictures **30-31** Culver Pictures
32 Hulton Getty/Liaison Agency **33** *Boy with a
Straw Hat Waiting to March in a Pro-War Parade*,
1967 Copyright © 1969 The Estate of Diane Arbus
LLC/The Museum of Modern Art, New York,
The Ben Schultz Memorial Collection, gift of the
photographer **34** New York *Herald Tribune*
35 FSA/Corbis **36** Black Star **36-37** Black Star
38 Contact Press Images **39** Contact Press Images

TO CAPTURE
42-43 Dallas *Times Herald* **44** New York *Daily News*
45 AP/Wide World Photos **46** Buffalo *Courier-
Express* **47** AP/Wide World Photos **50-51** Abraham
Zapruder ©LMH c/o Silverberg 1967, renewed 1995
52 AP/Wide World Photos **53** AP/Wide World
Photos **54-55** Contact Press Images **56-57** Magnum
Photos **57** AP/Wide World Photos **58-59** Saba Press
60-61 Corbis

TO CELEBRATE
62-63 Black Star **64-65** Magnum Photos **66** LIFE
Magazine ©Time Inc. **67** AP/Wide World Photos
68-69 Corbis/Ansel Adams Publishing Rights Trust
70-71 Stern/Black Star **72** Aurora **72-73** Aurora
76-77 Magnum Photos **77** Gamma Liaison
78-79 Contact Press Images

TO ADVOCATE
80-81 Magnum Photos **82-83** Courtesy George
Eastman House **84** FSA/Culver Pictures
85 Library of Congress **86-87** Black Star
88-89 W. Eugene Smith courtesy Black Star
90 Domestic Abuse Awareness **90-91** Magnum
Photos **92-93** Gamma Liaison **96-97** Sygma

TO RISK
98-99 Contact Press Images–Epicenter
Communications **100-101** Topham/The Image
Works **102** Magnum Photos **103** Magnum Photos
104 Magnum Photos **104-105** Magnum Photos
106-107 AP/Wide World Photos **108-109** Aurora
109 NGS Image Collection **110-111** Magnum
Photos **112-113** Reuters/Archive Photos
114-115 AP/Wide World Photos

TO EXPLORE
116-117 The Stock Shop/NASA **118-119** ©Royal
Geographic Society **119** ©Royal Geographic Society
120 ©Harold and Esther Edgerton Foundation,
1999, courtesy of Palm Press **121** Science Photo
Library/Photo Researchers **122-123** Woodfin Camp
123 Archive Photos **124** Albert Bonniers Forlag AB,
A Child Is Born, Dell Publishing Company
125 Albert Bonniers Forlag AB, *A Child Is Born*,
Dell Publishing Company **126** NASA **128** NASA
129 NASA **130-131** NGS Image Collection
132 NASA **132-133** NASA

TO REVEAL
135 Magnum Photos **136** Corbis **137** LIFE
Magazine ©Time Inc. **138** Magnum Photos
139 Corbis/Ansel Adams Publishing Rights Trust
140 ©Halsman Estate **141** ©Halsman Estate
142-143 CPi **143** CPi **146-147** Rare Air Media, Ltd.

TO CHEER
152-153 ©The Estate of Garry Winogrand, courtesy
Fraenkel Gallery, San Francisco **154** AP/Wide World
Photos **157** National Archives **158** AP/Wide World
Photos **158-159** Corbis **160-161** Hulton Getty
163 Allsport **166** SPORTS ILLUSTRATED ©Time Inc.
167 Allsport

INDEX BY PHOTOGRAPHER

U.S. OLYMPIC
TEAM BEATS
THE U.S.S.R.
IN HOCKEY,
2/22/80
Heinz Kluetmeier

Right:
**FLORENCE
GRIFFITH
JOYNER,
9/88**
Mike Powell

TO CHEER

FINISHING IN STYLE

In the memorable picture above, the U.S. Olympic hockey team celebrates a surprising
gold-medal win over the Soviet Union at the 1980 Winter Games at Lake Placid, N.Y. The
thrill was magnified because the Soviet team had already crushed a National Hockey
League all-star team, and had whipped the U.S. Olympic team in an exhibition game. The
American flag in the background brands the picture as an emblem of the cold war.

Long hair streaming, long nails glinting, long legs pumping , Florence Griffith Joyner
was a photo-op in motion every time she hit the track. The exuberant sprinter heralded
one of the century's most significant (and overdue) movements in sport: the ascendance
of women to take their place on the field, the court and the track. At the 1988 Olympics
in Seoul, "Flo-Jo" was in her dominating prime, winning three gold medals. But her
inspiring story had a sad ending: she died in 1998, at age 38, of cardiac arrest. In a
eulogy written for TIME, Olympic sprinter Gail Devers said, "She raised the standard of
competition and at the same time brought femininity to our sport. She showed by example
that when you look great, you feel great—and when you feel great, you perform great."

Browns were playing mudball with the Forty-Niners. Says Leifer: "This shot was photographed in 1963, when football was still played on real grass. You don't have to look very close to

imagine how much photographers miss the real grass as opposed to the AstroTurf, which so many of the major stadiums have today. By the time you got into the third or fourth

quarter, you couldn't miss. The players really looked like they were in a game." In those halcyon days of muck, the sportscaster's cliché—"gladiators of the gridiron"—used to ring true.

TO CHEER

WHEN MEN WERE MEN AND MUD WAS MUD

Noted sports photographer Neil Leifer had already shot many of the great athletes of the '60s and '70s when he joined the TIME staff in the 1980s. His best pictures from that era can be found in the book *Neil Leifer's Sports Stars* (Doubleday; 1985), including this image of the great, tough running back Jim Brown on a day when he and his Cleveland

FROM CHAMP'S VAMP TO CHUMP'S CHOMP

Muhammad Ali: he came, he bragged, he conquered our hearts. Once upon a time, the Parkinson's-afflicted specter who lit the Olympic torch in Atlanta in 1996 was the inimitable boxer named Cassius Clay. Here we see him in a Neil Leifer photo, crowing over a hapless Sonny Liston after knocking him out in the first round of their rematch for the world championship in 1965. That was the night when Liston went down so fast that fans in the arena began to chant, "Fix! Fix! ... Fake! Fake!"

Believe it or not, according to TIME's original account, the voluble youngster was initially at a loss for words to explain the seemingly phantom punch with which he had decked "the ugly bear." But before long he came up with a picturesque moniker for the mystery. The blow, he now insisted, had been his secret "anchor punch"—one so strong it anchored his foe to the canvas. Explained Clay: "It's a chop, so fast you can't see it. It's karate. It's got a twist to it. Just one does the job."

Sublime, but, as Napoleon said, it's a short step from the sublime to the ridiculous, and boxing has followed that sorry trajectory since Ali's glory days. We can pin a precise date on the sport's nadir: it came on June 28, 1997, when former heavyweight champ Mike Tyson resorted to unusual tactics when fighting good-guy Evander Holyfield in Las Vegas. Unable to beat Holyfield with his fists, Tyson took a big bite out of his opponent's ear. Winner: Holyfield. Loser: Tyson—and boxing.

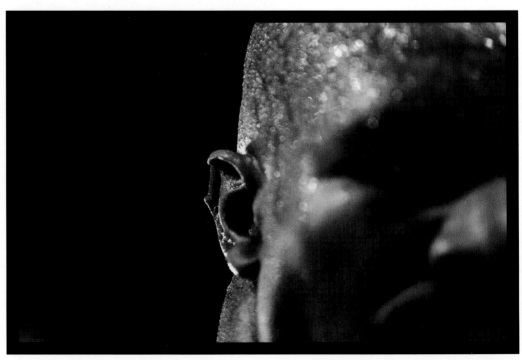

EVANDER HOLYFIELD,
6/28/97
Jed Jacobsohn